Never Again
by
Deri Rundle

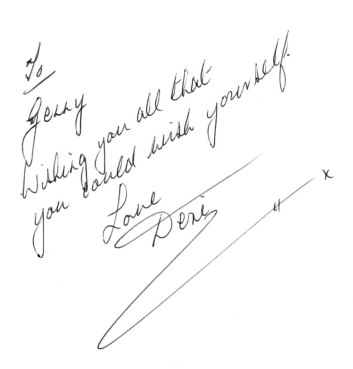

To
Gerry
Wishing you all that
you could wish yourself.
Love
Deri

x

RUNDLE
FRANCIS DRIVE
BIDEFORD   DEVON

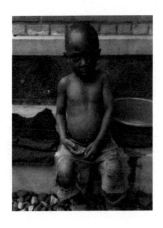

ISBN 978-0-9573101-0-0
Printed in Great Britain by
Arthur H. Stockwell Ltd
Torrs Park   Ilfracombe
Devon

*This book is dedicated to the memory of my
dear husband David and sister Rose
also to my daughter Leigh
for her invaluable help and constructive advice*

- - o o O o o - -

It seems that each of our small lives blend into the
history of the world much as drops of rain disappear into
the earth from which we came,
each with a certain entitlement,
the question being
what have we made of this time?
How have we developed and exercised our ability to
perceive, comprehend, appreciate and give accordingly
that modicum which was our share?
And oh! how precious, how painful, how beautiful
has been this little time lived
with so many dear people.

DJR

- - o o O o o - -

My sincere thanks to Terry Adams for his
untiring help in assembling this book and
to his wife Chris for the' loan' of Terry
on so many occasions

The main question asked during my talks about The David Rundle Trust and its work in Rwanda is, 'Why did a carnage such as the genocide take place?'

It's not essential that you read this chapter on the History of Rwanda as you will, no doubt, want to turn to page 11 where my story really begins. Nevertheless, by reading the few pages detailing Rwanda's recent history, it may help to put events described in the main body of the book into context.

Contents

Photographs   Pages   76 - 83

List of Abbreviations and Language   Page   169

Why I first went to Rwanda

My husband, David, and I had always supported children and animals but in his latter years he had suffered a long and disabling illness and was unable to continue with our work physically. Then one Tuesday evening - 20th April 1996 at ten minutes to midnight - he was gone! It was our daughter's birthday, David's the next day and mine on the 25th.

I would never have believed one human being could miss another so much.

Twelve months after David's death I was given the opportunity of working in the rain forests of Indonesian Borneo with orangutans and felt this would probably be my salvation. It was to be challenging, interesting, hard work and extremely time consuming.

During my time at Camp Leakey in Kalimantan I met a vet who had worked with the mountain gorillas in Rwanda. He painted a gruesome picture of the situation out there, mainly due to the genocide and ensuing war and, although in my sixties, I decided to accept the challenge and see the situation for myself. Unfortunately I was not fully prepared for the horrors and poverty that greeted me but could not turn my back on a people who were crying out for help in all directions especially for clean water.

The Dian Fossey Gorilla Fund (as it was then) aided my visit with the necessary contacts and I funded my first water tank project in Rwanda. On returning to the UK I realized it would be impossible to continue with this work unless I could raise further funding. This was the reason I decided to apply for charity status, was accepted, and The David Rundle Trust was born in memory of David.

Geography of Rwanda

Rwanda is a small, mountainous, volcanic country situated in central Africa and is bordered by four other African countries; to the west is the Democratic Republic of the Congo (formerly Zaire), to the north is Uganda, the east Tanzania and Burundi is on its southern borders. Set on the western branch of the East African Rift it's one of the poorest and most heavily populated countries in the world and subject to drought, famine, parasitic and other diseases. Its main exports are tea and coffee; the mountain gorillas are an enviable tourist attraction. Potatoes, plantains, maize, sorghum and beans are Rwanda's staple crops.

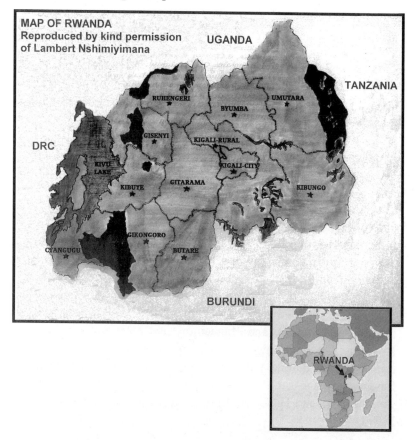

MAP OF RWANDA
Reproduced by kind permission of Lambert Nshimiyimana

*'Revolution is born of poverty that does not allow
the sharing of material wealth'*
Danziger's Travels

1994 Rwandan genocide and ensuing war

WHO? WHAT? WHERE and WHY?
We know WHO were the perpetrators of the genocide
We know WHAT they did
We know WHERE they did it
Do you know WHY they did it?

History of Rwanda

During the latter years Rwanda's history has been as predictable as most African countries, poverty, greed and outside influences having initiated many of its problems.

Most people have heard of Rwanda but very few know where it is situated on the African continent and have no idea what engineered the horrific genocide of 1994 and ensuing war.

The historically and socially marginalized Batwa (pygmy Twa), currently representing only 1% of Rwanda's population, were the earliest confirmed inhabitants of this central African country and lived for centuries in the dense rain forest region of the Great Lakes. They are the forebears of today's Hutus; the émigré Hamitic Tutsis allegedly emerging from the east African region.

Unfortunately, during conflicts, militants usually separated Hutu and Tutsi into class or caste rather than tribe or ethnicity. Rwandans agree the term Tutsi was used in pre-colonial Rwanda to represent a cattle keeper and therefore affluent; Hutu meant a less prosperous agricultural farmer; they spoke the same language and were known to switch tribes.

During the early 18th century border camps were guarded by a mix of Tutsi and Hutu these preventing incursions over their established but vulnerable borders. All tribes were united and served the powers of the Mwami (king). As early as the mid 18th century a political imbalance emerged with a Tutsi hierarchal system under the control of a Mwami. Gradually, during the late 19th century, this dynasty of

3

Rwandan pastoral Tutsi kings gained complete control of the agrarian Hutus.

In 1890 Germany claimed Rwanda as part of German East Africa but, at the end of World War I, Belgian forces administered Rwanda under the League of Nation's Mandate and Tutsis continued to influence the administration of the country.

Unfortunately, Belgium's policy of indirect rule, education of Tutsis in Catholic schools together with admiration of Tutsi leadership, widened the ethnic rift as did the issue of racial identification cards which legally defined Tutsi from Hutu.

Until colonisation Tutsi, Hutu and Batwa had lived together in propinquity and intermarriage was common. Many scholars and researchers argue that European and American influences led to the enmity and racial division between the Hamitic slender, thin nosed Tutsi and the contrasting stocky, broad nosed, darker skinned Hutu.

During their rule the avaricious Belgians established harsh laws and the population was continuously forced to grow ever larger quantities of coffee and tea to increase profits. The introduction of physical punishment, forced labour and an onerous corvée brought about the migration of hundreds of thousands of Rwandans to Uganda - at that time a British dependency.

The 1950's saw radical changes with the emasculation of Tutsis remaining in Rwanda. These were brought about by Belgium's, and the Catholic Church's, gradual uneasy observance of Hutu exploitation.

Mutara Rudahigwa, son of exiled King Yuhi Musenga, (King Yuhi had refused baptism and was therefore exiled) received seminary education and was baptised and renamed Charles. His political changes, and the Catholic Church's opposition to Tutsi domination of Hutus, allowed Hutus and Catholics into positions of authority. This resulted in Tutsis no longer enjoying the status of masters in Rwanda.

The once wealthy Tutsi's control of cattle and elevated social status slowly diminished and ethnic identity cards were again introduce, the data self-identifying as Hutu, Tutsi and Twa. Enormous gains were made by Hutus when secret ballots were introduced during elections.

Charles's liberal policies led to his assassination in 1959 and, despite King Kigihi's V's (Charles's son) valiant efforts, Civil War broke out stimulated by the Belgian military. King Kigihi, the last Rwandan monarch, fled to Uganda.

This gradual loss of power infuriated the Tutsis resulting in an assassination attempt being made in 1959 on the life of Gregoire Kayibanda, then leader of the (MDR) Movement Democratique Republicain, the largest Hutu political party at that time. Spasmodic genocide ensued with thousands of Tutsis being massacred by Hutus and many more escaping to neighbouring countries. These spates of violence, known as 'muyaga' (wind) stopped as suddenly as they started.

UN intervention resulted in a referendum which produced overwhelming support for a Republic and in 1961 Gregoire Kayibanda was declared Prime Minister of the first Rwandan Republic and the Parmehutu Party.

Rwanda gained independence from Belgium in 1962 and from then on power was completely Hutu and Catholic dominated; 150,000 Tutsi were exiled, the remaining Tutsis becoming scapegoats for the country's problems. The new Hutu Rwanda intended a complete break with its history of Tutsi supremacy.

Progress ensued, but so did corruption and inefficiency. Ethnic tensions intensified when unemployment peaked and Tutsis were allowed only 10% of school or university seats or civil service positions, they were described as inyenzi (cockroaches). In 1964 Hutus would not be prosecuted for murdering a Tutsi and this resulted in many more Tutsis fleeing as refugees.

Spasmodic calls from the West were made for intervention but were ignored. The issue of ethnicity remained powerful although domestic stability improved when serving Minister of Defence, Major General Juvenal Habyarimana deposed Gregoire Kayibanda in July 1973 and later formed the Movement Republicain National pour la Democratique et le Developpement (MRND).

Although Juvenal Habyarimana declared his objectives were to promote unity, peace and national development, state-sanctioned discrimination against Tutsis, both in schools and the workplace, remained and as sole candidate Habyarimana was re-elected in 1978/83 and 88.

In 1990 tensions were again unleashed, due to food shortages and a slump in the economy, and exiled Ugandan based rebels (FPR), many of whose members were Tutsis, began pressurising the Rwandan government for concessions and recognition of their rights as Rwandans. During sporadic fighting between the FPR and Hutu Government forces the FPR came very close to capturing Kigali the Rwandan capital.

Promises made by Habyarimana and his government for a National Political Charter, intending to help reconcile Hutus and Tutsi, never materialised and in October 1990 the FPR, in desperation, invaded Rwanda from their base in Uganda. French, Zairian and Belgian forces were brought in to repel them.

A cease-fire took effect in July 1992 and political talks ensued in Arusha, Northern Tanzania but, even after a coalition government was formed pending a general election, Tutsi and Hutu tension persisted and intermittent Tutsi cross border attacks resulted in extensive government and militia retaliation against Tutsis remaining in Rwanda.

Ethnic tensions reached critical levels and Habyarimana justified the establishing of genocidal pogroms, directed against Tutsis and any moderate Hutus, by proclaiming it was the Tutsis' intention to return Hutus to their previous degrading lifestyle and the Tutsi ethnic group to power.

Anti-Tutsi propaganda had been pumped out of the Mille Collins radio for several years, prior to that fateful day on April 6th, financed by businessmen in league with the Hutu government. Prominent Tutsis were often found slaughtered soon after a presenter had mentioned their names over the radio.

In April 1994 a Mystere-Falcon 50 jet, an expensive present from the French President to the Hutu Rwandan government, was shot down while preparing to land at Kigali airport with President Habyarimana and the President of Burundi on board. Habyarimana was burnt beyond recognition and, ironically, parts of his mangled plane came to rest in the grounds of his own mansion. The FPR had met with Habyarimana in Arusha the night before the crash but, unfortunately, the talks had collapsed. There were no survivors and RTLM (Radio-Television Libre des Mille Collins) instantly accused the Tutsis of the President's death.

Militia and Interahamwe immediately began capturing and killing Tutsis, moderate Hutus and opposition politicians including the

Prime Minister, Agathe Uwilingiyamana and her ten Belgian bodyguards.

It has never been established who fired the fateful shots which brought down the jet but there was never any doubt the genocide had been systematically planned in advance of this prophetic crash. The violence which followed the 6th April 1994 was one of the worst in the history of mankind.

The FPR claimed extremists amongst the President's Hutu guards had assassinated him whilst intending to stage a coup, whereas the government-backed Hutu Rwandan army (MRND) blamed the FPR.

France, Belgium and UN Security Consul withdrew their forces and America stated that the US Peacekeeping operations had to be 'in US interests' and, therefore, severely limited US funding and involvement in the peacekeeping mission

It has never ceased to amaze me the ease with which a never ending supply of weapons can be obtained by economically unstable and starving countries. Lorry loads of machetes and arms appeared as if by magic on the night of the 5th April 1994, the commencement of the real genocide.

From time immemorial man has installed emissaries, politicians, missionaries; supplied weapons to countries, clans and tribes throughout the world in order to loot and plunder resources such as gold, oil, slaves, palm oil, timber or to establish some strategic foothold – nothing has ever been sacred. Whatever Africa has to offer has always been sifted and its most profitable wealth taken.

It was estimated between April and July of 1994 over eighty thousand Tutsis and moderate Hutus were massacred by bands of militia and thugs calling themselves Interahamwe. The final count will never be known.

Neighbours, families, Hutu husbands and wives, priests, nuns and doctors were incited by officials to kill the inyenzi. Killings were also sanctioned, encouraged, even ordered by those in authority in Rwanda. Doctors exchanged their healing medical instruments for weapons in order to hack Tutsi men, pregnant women and their children to death; priests removed their dog collars and donned grenade neckties. Not all victims were shot, the majority were raped, tortured then bludgeoned to death. Why waste expensive ammunition?

Survivors were maimed both in body and mind for the remainder of their lives.

We all have to die but our death should not be of someone else's volition leaving behind a second generation incomplete and polluted who linger in this damaged state until their death.

Not all Hutus were monsters - many moderates paid dearly for their compassion towards Tutsis. One tenth of the Rwandan population died in one hundred days and Rwanda, supposedly a seriously religious country! Whatever happened to the commandments, 'Thou shalt not kill' and 'Love thy neighbour.'

Governments should not be judged by their words but by their deeds. For Rwanda, during the genocide, there were few words and no deeds. The governments and people of the western world settled themselves comfortably in their plush armchairs or nonchalantly swivelled on bar stools to watch a news flash on the television screen. Mutilated men and women lay still, many more knelt on the baked earth with hands clasped together pleading for mercy; children lay like broken dolls awaiting transport to a doll's hospital. The fortunate died quickly their dying whispers joining the night's breeze as it glided imperceptibly into the silent mountains.

The world saw, but did nothing.

In May 1994 the UN finally conceded, 'Acts of genocide may have been committed.' It was estimated by the Red Cross that Hutus and extremists were responsible for one hundred thousand deaths! Hutu Rwandans were directly responsible for the blood bath of 1994 but the western world was indirectly answerable.

Why are we not willing to recognise the suicide note history leaves?

In April 1994 Paul Kagame, Tutsi leader of the FPR forces based in Uganda, resumed Civil War against the Hutu Rwandan Government (MRND). The FPR, stationed at Kigali under the Arusha Accord, had come under attack immediately after the shooting down of President Habyarimana's plane but managed to fight its way out and join Paul Kagame's FPR forces in the north.

The FPR emerged victorious and in July 1994 some two million Hutu refugees, fearing Tutsi reprisals, fled to neighbouring countries, many to Zaire (DRC). The fleeing Hutu refugees died of starvation, cholera, dysentery and other diseases which swept the refugee camps, especially in Zaire where Civil War broke out in 1998.

The FPR, backed by Uganda, entered Zaire to flush out the defeated Hutu Interahamwe many of whom remain in the jungles of the DRC to this day. Their years have been spent not only raping and terrorising their own people in these camps but also the people of Democratic Republic of the Congo.

After the war thousands of Hutus laid down their arms and returned to Rwanda from their refugee camps. Many have been released after being 'tried' before a civilian Gecaca Court; victims, or relatives of victims, act as their judges. Others have been executed if proved guilty before a judicial court. Although many remain in prison the death sentence was abolished in 2007 and hardened criminals convicted of genocide, rape and gang related crimes now face life in solitary confinement. Unfortunately those remaining in the DRC would, no doubt, if given the opportunity wage war and genocide again.

Presidential and Legislative elections took place in August and September 2003 and Paul Kagame and the FPR political party was unanimously elected.

There are those who say God was absent during this slaughter in Rwanda and lives could have been saved but this is not so - there were many acts of charity far beyond the palls of altruistic bravery.

'We were not puppets and did not have to dance to the murderer's tune even when they tried to pull our imaginary strings,' said an elderly Hutu grandfather when relating his experiences to me one day.

The fate of many families was held in the balance during these terrible times and their stories are both horrifying and wretched.

Kaz, a boy of nine young years, had experienced the genocide and was soon to be catapulted into a life even an adult should not be expected to contemplate.

Chapter One

'The Greater the Obstacle, the More Glory in Overcoming it'
Moliére

Kaz - The Boy Soldier

The two boys were scouting in advance of the main body of men; young boys were small, light footed, quick - and expendable. There was an ear-shattering crack, the sound a machete makes when splitting a large log. At the same time ten year old Kaz was drenched, not with rain but warm blood. He was unable to focus his left eye and his long, bedraggled, dirty, black hair soon turned scarlet, as did parts of his stinking apology for a soldier's uniform.

An obnoxious stench filled Kaz's nostrils and on turning he realised his companion's head had been split open down to the nose by fire from the enemy. His first reaction was relief, it was not his blood gradually congealing on his sweaty, thin young body but that of his year long, close friend Obie.

A strangled gurgle was emitted from what remained of this eleven year old's mouth and his arms and war torn body twitched rapidly as though performing a ceremonial tribal death dance.

Kaz blasted a 180 degree arc of machine gun fire into a faceless enemy and uttered a silent prayer as he dropped to the forest floor. He was sure the enemy could hear his hammering heartbeats and quick, short gasps of breath. Why wouldn't Mother Nature allow the warm, damp earth to open and permit him to sink quickly, but silently, into her welcoming bosom?

A light tap on his foot brought Kaz back to reality. Without raising his head he twisted it slowly to the right amassing even more dirt and grime into his now bloodstained features. Army boots were inches from his body and the muzzle of a rifle tickled his ear. With eyes squeezed shut and a heart pounding he waited for the inevitable click of a safety catch to be released.

During and after the genocide children's suffering was horrifying and the canvas depicting the lives of Kaz, Pascal K, Alphonsine, Emmanuel, John, Pascal H and many others is part of a picture which needs to be painted.

Chapter Two

'Death lasted for minutes but the consequences for ever'

Kaz - In the Army

Another burst of machine gun fire sent splinters of bark from nearby trees in all directions. Kaz froze. Grenades were lobbed, followed by a scream, as the government troops took cover. There was no return fire from the rebels as the remaining government soldiers advanced cautiously. They found only two blood splattered children in uniform lying prostrate on the ground, one on its back with a head split in two the other lying face down with what looked like wounds to the head and left side of the body.

An eternity can be measured in a lifetime or a few seconds and it was not until he heard a gruff familiar voice rasp, 'Are they both dead?' Kaz realised it was his battalion commander - he was safe.

Soldiers in varying degrees of khaki uniform appeared in twos and threes. Some dropped on one knee, alert, with guns at the ready, others spread out for cover amongst the towering forest trees.

The gun no longer pointed at Kaz's pulsating temple and he rolled away from the blood spattered log anxious to join his comrades. Two men dragged the pitiful body of Obie into the trees.

Spasmodic machine gun fire could be heard in the vicinity and then an explosion. Clods of earth, wood splinters and shrapnel showered the men sending them flat on their faces, hands and arms automatically whipping up to cover their unprotected heads. One wiry, seasoned soldier was wounded in the arm and a baby faced teenager's leg, from the thigh to knee, resembled a miniature, erupting volcano as it pulsed a rainbow of blood and shredded flesh from around its perimeter.

Babyface clapped a hand over his mouth to prevent himself from screaming and the other instinctively went down to his wounded leg. A right hook to Babyface's jaw rendered him unconscious – silence was essential. Strong hands buried themselves in his sweat soaked armpits and he was dragged from his exposed position; the commander gave a silent signal to retreat.

Babyface was lifted over the shoulder of a weary comrade who quickly disappeared heading towards their hastily assembled HQ a short distance away; Kaz refused to leave Obie. 'Your mate's dead boy, come on or you'll soon join him, we've no time for sermons and burials,' he was told.

Kaz crawled over to where Obie was lying spread eagled on his back, his body still warm and supple. He held the warm hand and was sure the fingers made an effort to clasp his but what remained of Obie's once tired, welcoming eyes now remained closed. Their comrades had disappeared as silently as they had come and Kaz was alone. He knew any sound might be heard by the enemy so lay beside the body and tried to decide whether to take Obie with him or endeavour to return to the make-shift head quarters alone.

There was a strong smell of cordite hanging in the air but no sound other than the breeze beating a tattoo through the tops of tall trees. Kaz heaved Obie onto his shoulders and, when no further gunfire ensued, he made for the HQ.

His comrades were busily gathering together their stores of diminishing ammunition and food, making ready to move out so Kaz had no alternative but go with them. Obie was thrown down a shallow bog pit for there was no time to give him a dignified burial.

Kaz was weary, dirty, hungry, thirsty and heavy hearted for Obie was his best friend and the third boy they'd lost that week. With torrid tears burning his bleary eyes he stood for a few seconds, looking down at the broken body sprawled in the bottom of the fetid pit, before joining his fellow soldiers.

Life would never be the same again for Kaz.

Chapter Three

'Adopt the pace of nature, her secret is patience'
Ralph Waldo Emerson

My First Flight to Rwanda

Like Kaz, my life would never be the same again after my first visit
to Rwanda. It began from my home county - Devon - then via
Heathrow and Nairobi to Kigali the capital of Rwanda.

As I was to spend the next three months working in Rwanda
Kenyan Airways had allowed me an extra 23 kilograms so I was
carrying a twenty three kilogram hold all, a pretty hefty backpack
and hand luggage.

On entering Heathrow I found an empty bench and decided to sit
down and familiarize myself with the extremely busy surroundings.
As soon as I moved my posterior towards the seat I knew I was in
trouble. The weight of the backpack moved the centre of gravity
and, before touching down, I found my body - and backpack - moving
backwards at a fair rate of knots eventually sending me base over
apex! Unfortunately I couldn't get up and lay there like a stranded
upturned turtle. Several people came to my assistance trying not to
smile, helped me remove my backpack and place me into an upright
position. What a way to begin my journey!

Economy flight number K101 to Kigali was not one of the most
comfortable journeys I have experienced. Sandwiched between
a grey-haired, bespectacled, elderly gentleman, who was obviously
mid-way between influenza and pneumonia, and an extremely
talkative young women with a precocious three year old meant rest,
reading or relaxation for the next nine hours were impossible

Directly behind me a further four seats were occupied by the
father and three more siblings who were determined to disrupt as
many passengers as possible. They continually kicked the backs of
seats, leaned over and pulled their mother's hair or punched and
teased their youngest brother who squirmed beside the irate mother
in his efforts to extricate himself from her grasp – no doubt with
retaliation in mind.

Our first meal was served and this brought a short respite, but not for long; each child had likes and dislikes and, although the father made every effort to stop them, the brothers passed any unwanted food to the mother and youngest child. He ate everything, including his brothers' leftovers, with the consequence the food eaten at 9pm returned at 9.30pm!

The patience of the cabin crew was exemplary and with the mother and son in the toilet for the next twenty minutes everything quieted down.

The harassed mother returned with a noiseless and very pale son wrapped like a papoose in a Kenyan airline blanket. Fortunately, being a night flight, the other children finally exhausted themselves and at least twenty adjacent passengers heaved a sigh of relief when the youngest sucked the sleeve of his teddy bear's jumper and, with a few whimpers, relaxed on his mother's lap into what we hoped would be a long sleep.

I noticed the cabin attendants slowed down and passed our seats on tiptoe during the night no doubt endeavouring to avoid any sound that might disturb the dear little people.

There were two other incidents of any consequence; the five year old wet his pants about 3am prompting our compartment to submerge further into their seats and draw blankets over their heads hoping the disturbance would be brief; and the eldest brother fell down the aeroplane steps when disembarking. Myself and several other passengers left via another exit so we were not sure whether anything was broken but we could hear the victim was certainly not dead.

I hoped these experiences weren't an omen for my first night in Rwanda!

Chapter Four

*'Courage is the art of being the only one who knows
you're scared to death'*

Earl Harold Wilson

My First Night on Rwandan Soil

Being my first visit to this beautiful, mountainous country I had much to learn. One needs a good sense of humour, patience in abundance and able to adjust very quickly to using little water.

Although there have been many happy, frightening, interesting and unforgettable experiences during my times in Africa, my first night on Rwandan soil proved the most memorable.

Before leaving the UK I obtained the telephone number of the only hotel I could find in the town of Ruhengeri so telephoned from Kigali Airport, booked a room and arrived with high expectations. The hotel's postage stamp grass patch was well tended and the entrance welcoming but its pot bound palms struggled to breathe and expand for want of space and water. Several varied coloured people and two Mzungus stood chatting in reception, others waited by their four by four cruisers until their black drivers had unloaded luggage and everyone was ready to follow a porter to the respective chalet rooms.

A single wicker chair, placed conveniently just inside the door of reception, was unoccupied so I sat and waited for the crowd to disperse before walking to the desk and giving my name. The receptionist greeted me with a broad smile, bent over his desk, and ran his index finger down what I presumed was a list of bookings which lay before him. Having reached the bottom of the list he raised his head and asked me to spell my name. This I did and he repeated the finger exercise only to find I was not listed. The once smiling receptionist's countenance now carried a deep crease between the bushy black eyebrows. His pursed lips issued a hissing sound then, turning to his colleague seated at an adjacent table, he spoke quietly in what I assumed was Kinyarwanda. Initially the two close shaven heads nodded then shook in a negative fashion before informing me all the rooms had been taken by a delegation representing charity agencies.

'Does this mean I have no bed in which to sleep?' I asked, 'Isn't there a single bed available in any of the rooms?' Profuse apologies ensued and I was informed enquiries would be made so I returned to the wicker chair and waited, my stomach churning slightly both from hunger and apprehension. Twenty long minutes later a tall, serious faced black man appeared and stood before me holding out his hand in greeting. He introduced himself as the manager and it was obvious he was extremely embarrassed at having to inform me, in French, 'There are several twin-bedded rooms in which there is only one person but no one from the relief agency is prepared to double up or give you a bed.' He advised me to try a mission a little further down the road. At this stage had I carried a tent I would have happily pitched it on the postage stamp patch of green grass with or without permission.

Dusk was falling as I eventually reached the mission after stumbling over several hundred yards of mud and rubble with a full pack. A stocky, shabbily dressed man appeared behind me as I neared the building and escorted me to an opening, the wooden door having been ripped from its hinges and left propped up at an angle against the rukarakara wall. The stench that emanated from this opening did not instil confidence but I had no alternative but to go inside and find a resting place until morning when I could make my way to the village in which I would be working.

The building was occupied and I was met by several tall, severe looking, black soldiers in varying modes of dress - and undress - some partially uniformed, others with a towel around their lower limbs and one stark naked. He stood paralysed for a few seconds then instinctively crossed both hands in front of his crotch before turning and whipping them over his buttocks, swivelling his head to take another look at the apparition, before disappearing rapidly through an open door. He was certainly more shocked than I; by this time I was prepared for anything!

Finally I was ushered along a dark corridor into a small dingy room and it was immediately obvious this was no five star celebrity pad. A curtain rail, minus curtains, sloped precariously across a grey cracked window for it had only the right hand support, the other rested listlessly on a dirty wooden floor. There was no lock on the

17

door its mechanism having long since been removed as had the handle.

My room attendant indicated with an outstretched hand towards the bed, muttered something in what I presumed was Kinyarwanda, and then held up the middle finger and half his index finger on his right hand. This, I thought, must be the price of a night's stay, perhaps one and a half of something. I prayed my presumption was correct and that I was not expected to pay in kind, although I did have a large box of condoms for the birth control group I hoped to organise and may have been able to begin my tuition that night. Finally I nodded and, luckily, the janitor disappeared.

I returned to the corridor and found two dimly lit light bulbs swinging from a bullet pitted ceiling and a shower that dribbled cold water onto dead cockroaches, the remainder of the plumbing had been pulled, or blasted, from the walls. The toilet facilities were even worse than some of the holes in the ground I had experienced previously in Uganda and Kenya.

Night descends quickly near the equator; it was now dark and I was bursting for a pee. I waited until all was quiet before I ventured outside and found a secluded corner. Unfortunately, during my squat, I peed in my boots. 'What the hell' I muttered. 'My feet needed washing anyway!'

On my return I tried the light switch not really expecting a response from the single bulb hanging limply in the centre of the ceiling; I was not disappointed! My ever faithful minute LED torch was still securely attached to my wrist by its elasticised strap and with the light from this I could clearly see the camp bed, the stability of which I gingerly tested not wanting to disappear into an abyss during a nightmare at two o'clock in the morning. There was a grey and, what had once been, white striped lumpy mattress whose stuffing erupted from several craters; no pillow but one gaudy, unctuous smelling blanket thrown onto the rickety resting place. These items proved to be the entire contents of the room apart from several reddish brown bodies scuttling under the bed as I flashed my torch around. These I left to their own devices for cockroaches, if squashed, turn slimy and emit an obnoxious smell.

By now I was wide awake and already experiencing aberrations; I was hungry, thirsty, angry and exceedingly lonely. Then I remembered a lifeline secreted somewhere in the depths of the much travelled, green canvas hold-all propped against the door. After much searching I found my late husband's battered, leather bound, brandy flask in which I hoped the much needed stimulant remained intact.

My fingers were stiff and swollen from forty eight hours of travelling, excessive heat and carrying a full pack, and I found it difficult to unscrew the small metal cap. Eventually the cap moved. Placing the flask to my lips I took a long hard pull and experienced a seductive tingling sensation as the velvety brown liquid seeped into my mouth, disinfected my un-cleaned teeth, trickled slowly to the back of the tongue, passed where tonsils had once rested, finally extending a warm glow to the whole of a fatigued old body. I lay on the bed, slipped into my sleeping bag still fully clothed, apart from the boots and urine soaked socks, and actually fell into a deep sleep.

I was awakened at dawn by an American army style repetitive chorus being belted out by armed Rwandan soldiers and their prisoners as they passed my grimy but now sun filled window. Many of these men - and women - were awaiting trial due to their involvement in the genocide but now, clothed in carnation pink prison uniforms in the form of short sleeved shirts and knee length shorts, the men repeated their guard's aria and kept a metronomic, bare foot running pace along the track, the billowing dust swirling like a morning mist as I watched them disappear into the haze.

I unzipped the sleeping bag, swung my legs out of bed and reluctantly decided, as there was no possibility of a hot cuppa, it would have to be nuts and dried fruit for breakfast plus a spoonful of marmite and a malaria tablet. The mosquitoes had been busy in the night and made a meal of both my arms! My luggage always includes dried milk, fruit and nuts, energy bars, tea, coffee, hot chocolate, biscuits, packets of soup and marmite. What would I do without my marmite! I'm informed it's rich in vitamin B12 and, therefore, a deterrent against mosquitoes as well as being extremely tasty and essential at the end of a long hot day when the body is craving salt.

In sanguine mood I was still alive but relinquished all rights to a bath, shower or even a cursory wash so, with breakfast devoured, I was ready to face whatever the day had to offer. Optimistically I hoped it was going to be better than my first night in Rwanda for there were water tanks to build and pipelines to install.

Chapter Five

'When you go out to seek revenge, dig two graves'
Chinese Proverb

Kaz - Family History

Kaz's paternal family were Hutus, their identity cards confirmed the fact as did their flattened nose bridge and flared nostrils, stocky stature and black skin, that is apart from Kaz and his mother.

Although not tall for his age Kaz's body portrayed a similarity to the slender Hamitic people originating in east Africa for he displayed their sharper features and lighter skin colour.

Benice, Kaz's mother, had been the envy of many during her teenage years and was pursued by men from her village and farther afield. Hamitic attributes had not manifested themselves in Benice to a degree that anyone suggested she was from Tutsi stock but her beauty and stature far outshone that of her peers.

When Kaz neared the age of two his father, John, began casting aspersions regarding Kaz's appearance and Benice's fidelity. Nothing could be proved and John decided the genetic difference must have been caused by an indiscretion committed by Benice's mother. He never forgave his wife for having a mother who had possibly had a relationship with an inyenzi (cockroach) and his dislike of Kaz and Benice turned to hatred over the years.

April 6th, the onset of the genocide, saw John the leader of a group of Interahamwe and, in one day, he killed fourteen people. He remembered one was a baby and perhaps two were young children but couldn't recall how many were men and women, he could only remember the ecstatic frenzy with which he had satisfied his hate for Tutsis. His actions proved to all who knew him that his serious intentions were to rid Rwanda of 'this filth - these inyenzis.' John never once thought that the baby he had stabbed to death had once looked innocently into his eyes as it bounced on his lap, chuckling as it curled its chubby fingers around his. The children he killed had played with his children and he had worked, sung and shared sorghum with the men and women while planting crops on the mountain sides.

Ambling along the road, carpeted either side with intricate shapes and colours forming an ever changing pattern of what once had been human beings, John sneered at the eyeless head resting in the fork of a banana tree and kicked a torso whose legs rested in near enough proximity to the body to give the impression of a circus entertainer on stilts.

He thought of returning home to deal with his wife and son; John had by no means sated his predatory lust for vengeance on all Tutsis for dealing him a wife and child with possible Tutsi blood running through their veins. But a report from his comrades in arms was also needed, and a possible top up of sorghum, before attending to this personal matter.

Bleary eyed, dishevelled, raucous thugs, with radios blaring out news and music from Mille Collins Radio Network, met John on the road and had no problem in persuading him to join them in another round of slaughter. John was leader of this gang.

A battery operated radio lay beside two bodies, both having been hacked beyond recognition. It had been dropped by the Interahamwe who found he needed two hands on the machete handle to complete his artwork.

Mille Collins news bulletins bellowed from another radio resting on a blood stained shoulder urging, 'Death to all inyenzis.'

Frenzied Hutus mockingly brandished machetes and nail-studded clubs at one another then continued their butchery of Tutsis who could do nothing but pray they would die quickly or soon awake to find they had experienced an horrendous nightmare.

Having breakfasted on looted alcohol and replaced their grenade necklaces around unwashed necks, the Interahamwe's slaughter continued throughout the day. A machete struck its fourth blow and a mother breathed her last, suffering no more. A woman found hiding in a ditch with two men, all carrying Hutu registration cards, were suspected of helping Tutsis so were dispatched; a further three human beings breathed their last, their final entreaties struggling from blood stained lips.

And so it went on.

All it needed was a slug of sorghum and a change of clothing to transform a pastor into a killer with grenades around his neck instead of his clerical dog collar, or a white coated doctor into a murderer with a machete where once he had held a stethoscope.

Dusk found John and many of the Interhamwe and militia exhausted but ready to leave the 'abattoir' and exchange notes with their comrades from other villages en route. They were eager to replenish their containers with banana or sorghum beer and boast how many 'cockroaches' had been squashed that day.

When human predators vacated their hunting grounds at dusk, carrion moved on to a table already spread for yet another banquet. With bloody beaks and gorged crops they pranced about one another, squawking and flapping their wings, fighting amongst themselves for the choicest morsels. Then finally, after taking a few tentative hops, lumbered into the air to find a quiet roosting place in which to digest what now filled their bloated bellies.

The torched, thatched huts offered up their dead and dying to grieving relatives who had been too frightened to venture down from the hills in broad daylight, even though some were Hutus.

As the night's breeze sauntered through the villages, now quiet after the ghoulish festivities of the day, it encountered and mingled with the bewildered ephemeral whispers of the day's victims, then joined in the momentum and urgency of the living whisperers searching for their slaughtered relatives. This gentle phantom momentarily rose and peeped quickly through burnt doors then swept down brushing reverently over charred and mutilated bodies as though administering their last rights.

Very many thousands were slaughtered for no apparent reason. 'It was a though we were taken over by the devil,' a grieving relative told me one evening when recounting his experiences of the genocide. The speed and scale of the massacre left even some Hutus reeling.

These victims had all once lived, many in poverty and hunger but were important to the world and had, like people in the western world, experienced passionate, intimate and loving relationships until the genocide when eyes, arms, legs, breasts and so many private parts of the human body were used by John and his thugs for rape, torture and butchery.

Many genocide victims were buried without shroud or coffin but remain in the memories of their loved ones and, perhaps, in the conscience of some of their torturers and murderers. There are no name plaques over which foreign visitors can cast their cursory glances, but sometimes large slabs of concrete under which thousands of grandmothers, children, fathers, mothers, aunts and uncles lie; churches and genocide museums where skeletons, still clothed in their ragged remains, wait for judgement day.

Kaz's father was killed in a fight over the possession of items plundered from massacred Tutsis. His team mates felt they should have had a bigger share of the loot, John thought otherwise. After a drunken brawl he was found sprawled on his back at the rear of his hut killed by a blow to the back of the head. At least his murderers had the decency to return the body to his wife.

Benice and the children heard a disturbance during the night but had been too frightened to venture outside so did not find John until dawn; wild dogs had taken their toll as had the early rising carrion. He was buried without ceremony in a shallow grave with the help of Hutu neighbours.

The interahamwe were slaughtering anyone who displeased them or whose answers were garbled, whose movements were too slow when food was demanded of them; no one was safe especially those related to, or connected with, Tutsis.

The need for flight soon became obvious, even to moderate Hutus, for there was a very strong possibility of savage revenge as the rebel army (FPR) gained superiority.

Chapter Six

'Once you have faced the impossible only the possible remains'
Kashmiri myth

Kaz – Trek to Zaire and Refugee Camp

The horrendous slaughter continued throughout April and May but in June the FPR's move south left the Hutu population, both moderates and Interahamwe, no alternative but to escape from Rwanda for they knew retribution was taking place as the FPR advanced.

After John's death Benice began a hoarding process, a corn cob here, a few grains of sorghum there. This was not easy as they were on the verge of starvation; the military and Interahamwe took what little food there was available.

Benice and five of her children packed what little they had and joined the never ending stream of Hutus making for the Zaire border hoping to find peace and a little security. The older members of the family had not been seen for weeks so Benice prayed they were not involved in the massacre and had escaped over the border earlier.

Many died during this trek, including one of Benice's children, for it was a journey of exhaustion, thirst, hunger and disease. She had no hoe with which to bury him so off loaded her few possessions onto the other children, who were already burdened with the few items they had managed to salvage, and carried her dead son until she found a shaded spot. They covered the gaunt body with leaves and branches, knelt down, prayed and wept, then continued their journey to what was to be another hell on earth.

Once in Zaire Benice gathered what remained of the family together and slept from shear exhaustion with the sound of crying children and moaning adults in her ears. They huddled together, arms about one another, to keep warm and initiate comfort.

Hours later Kaz awakened his mother. 'Mama, I'm thirsty Mama, please I want water.'

All around them, in the early morning mist, there were thousands of refugees who faced a future too overwhelming to contemplate. Some were fitfully sleeping others had died during the night. A few attempted to light fires and cook what little food they had in their battered pots; many sat on the sun baked earth and rocked back and forth wailing as they held their dust grimed heads in calloused hands and silently mourned dead family members lying beside them. A vacant-eyed women walked around with a dead baby in her arms, another strapped to her back, the heads of both were still able to nod as rigor mortis had not yet set in.

During the night a storm advanced slowly over the mountains from the north and black billowing clouds deposited their contents onto the sad bedraggled victims below.

The soil had been parched for days so could not digest the downpour turning the ground, first into a river and then a quagmire; the refugees moved about like geckos trapped in a sea of mud. Many thanked God as every available utensil able to hold liquid was turned to the heavens, as were wide open parched lips as they ingested the life giving nectar.

Children, who hours before had been weary little scraps of humanity, danced and ran about naked slipping and sliding as their tiny, sore feet squelched about on the playground floor.

As evening emerged a gaunt, bedraggled mother carrying her black cooking pot tapped Bernice on the shoulder and asked for food but Bernice had nothing to give her.

The mother retreated a few yards away and called her four children to her. 'I have a lovely coloured blanket here,' she told them. 'Now we have water this will make you a nourishing soup, but it will take some time to cook so you must all go to sleep and I will wake you when it's ready.'

The children watched as she tore the blanket into small pieces and placed them in her cooking pot. She had no dry wood so could not light the fire but she encouraged the children to settle down while she went to find kindling. Anxiously they cuddled close to one another on a piece of torn plastic but shivered as the sun set and the cold night air attempted to perturb their numbed, hungry bodies. The promise of food in their distended bellies helped to ease their troubled minds but their sleep was sporadic and uneasy.

The mother didn't return, she was found dead two days later on the perimeter of the camp, eagle sized raptors having enjoyed yet another banquet.

These refugee camps became a stinking, death riddled hell for thousands, the skin on their bones clinging more by habit than necessity; their bodies not yet ready to migrate from this world for they were not sure what the next world would hold Sunday sermons having repeatedly instilled into them there was hell, as well as Heaven, in the hereafter.

The defeated Interhamwe controlled the teeming refugee camps of mainly ethnic Hutus located across the Rwandan border in Zaire but, within a short time of arriving at the camp Kaz's days were spent in the ranks of a dishevelled army. Young boys were taken daily by force from the rat infested camps in Zaire (DRC) and trained at Nyiragongo then returned at night for feeding. This proved farcical for there was no food at the camps!

During this time it was the women and children who suffered most, what little food they had was seized and women were continually raped when they foraged for fire wood outside the camp.

Kaz failed to return one night and spent the next two years as a boy soldier. Reared by, and now separated from, his religious family Kaz found it impossible to understand or accept the genocide and war. Where was Kaz's God now?

Aid agencies finally arrived with limited assistance but much of the food meant for the starving masses disappeared before it reached the refugee camps and was sold on the black market or looted and eaten by those who already enjoyed three meals a day.

The violence and its memory have continued to affect Rwanda and its people, as well as the surrounding areas of Africa, to this day.

Although great strides have been made in education, birth control and the building of hotels, schools and new roads there is still much poverty in Rwanda and many other African countries. Civil and military strife is also prevalent throughout the continent and this promotes hunger and disease. Extensive research is essential before finance, or aid of any kind, is sent to these countries in order that:-

a) It reaches the people for whom it was intended

b) It can, and will be used, by the people for whom it was intended; what is the use of a lorry load of spades for people who have no shoes and work with hoes; sacks full of tin plates, mugs etc., for people who craft their own and really need food and blankets?

Chapter Seven

'We must rise above the gravitational pull of politicians,
their politics, greed and power'

Kaz is wounded

To be a boy soldier at ten years of age and sleep on the bare earth with a gun as your constant companion; to have killed and been near death oneself; to go days without proper food and have a gnawing hunger for ever in the pit of one's stomach - these are experiences a boy of ten years of age should not have to encounter but Kaz had and was still confronting these traumas.

Two of the guards stationed on the periphery of the temporary barracks brought their rifles into a firing position for one of them had detected a sound of twigs snapping then - silence. The taller of the two stabbed a forefinger at his colleague - **you** – then another quick stab with the same finger pointing into a northerly direction. The soldier obeyed the instructions immediately and, with shoulders hunched and head down, he circled round. A whisper emanated from his left, it sounded like the company's password. Cautiously he moved forward lifting and placing each foot in slow motion on the dry undergrowth; half sitting, half lying was a badly wounded 'runner' from his battalion. The news he carried was crucial if the men were to survive.

The rebel's strong force was close and what remained of Kaz's extremist Government Hutus were to make their way to Kinshasha in an endeavor to join a larger contingent. It was to be a long, hard three week march.

His company commander barked out commands and Kaz, who had been on night guard duty with three other seasoned soldiers, had to be ready to march immediately.

Life was hard and no allowances made for age - young or old - but the commander, although a strict disciplinarian, made sure the young boys had their fair share of what food was available and were not ill treated by his men.

Food was scarce and the boys scouted daily in search of anything edible, including plants, leaves and roots to replenish the rapidly diminishing food and medical supplies. It was during one of these sorties that Emmanuel stepped on a mine and was killed instantly. Kaz being immediately behind him, was caught in the blast and sustained shrapnel wounds to both legs.

The dead boy was left in the forest and two comrades, who were taller than Kaz, slung his arms over their shoulders, lifted his feet off the ground, and 'walked' him to a spot where their commander had called a temporary halt.

There was no field hospital or doctor; the commander cleaned and dressed the wounds. By the time the squad moved the next day, just before dawn, a rough stretcher had been made from plaited fronds and two good stout branches from a tree in order that Kaz could be carried for periods during the day's march.

By this time Babyface's leg was healing enough for him to be walking wounded so he accompanied Kaz for a couple of days while Kaz limped along; no one could stay an invalid for long, they impeded the company's movements and had to either improve quickly or stay behind and fend for themselves.

Often, during this grueling trek, planes were heard overhead and the men would immediately spread out and take cover to avoid detection. Ground cover was sometimes sparse, so initiative was essential; many men went into a hand stand at the nearest tree and stayed in this position until the danger passed. Being upside down, heads touching the ground with their bodies flat against the trunk and legs wrapped around the stock, meant they were difficult to spot.

Bomb attacks killed thousands and left many more injured. Often the commanders used their hand pistols to shoot those unable to walk; it was well documented, that with revenge on their minds, the rebels may torture and certainly kill any stragglers.

Malaria and other diseases were rife and many of the refugees they met en route were left where they lay because they were too weak to walk. Men from Kaz's company, together with thousands from all sides of this horrendous and seemingly endless war, were bombed, ambushed, shot, maimed and killed during the fighting and treks to refugee camps.

At twelve years of age Kaz had experienced some of the most savage fighting of the war and had carried out his share of slaughter. It was not only his legs that bore scars, his mind played tricks as he slept fitfully experiencing again and again the repeated horrors of the genocide and war. Often a punch in the ribs from a colleague, or his own screams, awakened him from these demonic depths.

In Warikale, a large forest in the Congo, pygmies (Batwa), wearing no clothes or just loin cloths and carrying spears, surveyed the soldiers from trees but, within a short time, were helping the battalion to build bridges from vines and catch insects and centipedes to roast. Many of the men suffered from disease and malnutrition and the younger boys, together with Kaz and a senior boy Robert, were often ordered to scout the forest for medical supplies. It was on such an occasion, hungry and thirsty, they set out before dawn keeping a sharp lookout for the enemy having been made aware by their commander that several central African countries had joined the fray initiating a convoluted situation. A partner and friend one day could easily become your enemy the next.

The sun's rays gradually warmed their tired bodies and soon a profusion of Inyabarasamya and Umutagara was gathered, excellent for treating wounds, plus Umubirizi, a good antidote for worms, was finally found before they rested to eat a few edible forest plants growing beside a trickle of water from the previous day's rain. Their medical supplies were tied together with young vines and placed in the shallow water along side tired, gnarled feet, while Robert quietly reminisced about his visits to an uncle's farm in Kisoro, Uganda when he was a child.

'We had milk to drink from his cows, clean mats and soft blankets for sleeping and were free to play in the fields once our chores were finished. My aunt and uncle had no children of their own but they made our family very welcome.'

This group of young heroes listened intently and all agreed how wonderful it would be to live in such a home.

Chapter Eight

'Now they belong with the ages'
Abraham Lincoln

Hero's Day

Hero's Day, the first of February, is an annual festive occasion in Rwanda which incorporates thanksgiving for the brave souls who fought and died for their country. Schools, universities, shops, offices, planters of crops, carers of goats, all Rwandans in fact enjoy a day from manual labour on Hero's Day.

Thousands will travel great distances to enjoy this special day on any mode of transport they can solicit, but the majority will have begun their journey before dawn on their trusty steeds - two feet. On the heads of most women will be hand woven, protuberant baskets packed with whatever is available for this special family day out, some hiding mundane luxuries covered with gaily checked cloths, others pretending.

The navy blue uniformed, armed police are in attendance as the crowds assemble at the gates to the arena but this is usually a day of good humour and camaraderie so they will be able to keep their guns safely shouldered. The dignitaries arrive and wave to the crowds through open car windows and once they are settled in comfortable chairs on the stadium the fun begins.

An abundance of the male population is always in evidence and, like the women, gathers in segregated groups to watch the entertainment, discuss their personal and the country's problems and, more importantly where, during their journey home, they will drink to the heroes of the past and present. Several will wake with sore heads and not just from the sorghum or banana juice.

Every school is represented and enters the arena with a standard bearer declaring the school's name. The drums beat faster and cheers ascend as the individual standards pass before the dignitaries.

Children are dressed in school uniforms; girls usually in blue dresses that will fit them for the next five years as they reach nearly to their ankles, others are obviously pass-me-downs riding well above the knees and bursting at the seams. Unfortunately, the boys, in beige shorts and shirts, experience the same difficulties as the girls and some shorts have to be secured with string if decency is to be observed. The teenagers are usually better equipped; the girls' skirts and blouses pristine their uniforms having been washed well in advance of the event; the long trousers of the male students distinguishing the men from the boys.

It's heart-wrenching to watch the youngsters' marching feet housed in an ill fitting array of shoes, boots, sandals and anything else that will pass for footwear. Many have not worn such luxuries before and find it difficult to hobble in step with the drum's beat and, at the same time, endeavour to keep their new found friends ensconced on their blistered feet. Several fall over, having lost their foot ware, and have to run with boot or shoe in hand in order to catch up and continue in the parade with one bare foot and a definite limp.

After the children's parade the workforce and retailers advertise their wares. The taxi firms arrive with highly polished transport which, unfortunately, shows the areas where ill matching paint has been quickly dabbed to cover bumps and bruises, and posters plastered to hide cracked windscreens.

Builders' lorries, needing a de-coke, belch out puffs of black exhaust fumes choking the crowds and the labour force waving from the back of offending vehicles. One newly painted, ancient lorry decides the parade is just too much and is having to be coaxed to the side. In the driving seat is a scowling boss whose sweating employees are having to push from the rear. Their perspiration is not just from the 80 degree sun but from the thought of docked wages for not making sure the old girl was in a fit condition to at least make it round the arena.

The Women's Co-operatives march along proudly carrying their beautifully crafted baskets and inevitable sleeping back packs, followed by the pièce de résistance; battalions of extremely smart, well rehearsed soldiers and military police, feet and arms all in unison and heads snapping round and saluting when approaching the dignitaries' podium.

The drummers drum, the marchers march, the advertisers advertise and this takes at least two hours before the real entertainment begins.

The older children and university students display their gymnastic prowess watched by prominent government officials, local leaders and six thousand excited onlookers, while hordes of young, raucous children, accompanied by their sedate mothers many attired in brightly coloured, traditional Rwandan dress, enjoy their freedom in safety; the inevitable sleeping babies strapped to their mothers' backs ignorant of the sacrifices made on their behalf by Rwanda's Heroes

The girls' artistry and balance when dancing are both phenomenal and beautiful. The exquisitely coloured, diaphanous material draped around their erotic bodies floats in unison with the swaying of their arms which snake out encouraging their male partners to succumb to their entreaties.

There are always one or two exceptional drummers who are allowed a solo spot; their act has the audience dancing in the aisles; their drum sticks move with such speed and precision they form a confusion of apparitions cutting through the astonished air.

No celebration would be complete without the dramatic lion dancers whose maned heads swivel right and left on glistening black shoulders with every hypnotic beat of the varying sized, hand carved wooden drums.

The speeches are usually long but, presumably, appreciated for there is much spontaneous clapping and I have never seen any hand boards popping up saying, 'Clap now' or 'Stop clapping.'

Once the speeches and entertainment draw to a close there are usually no handshakes as the dignitaries leave, but 'arm wrestling' hugs ensue and one's cheeks make contact with a recipient's alternative cheeks three times and foreheads knock gently together before taking one's leave - or as a welcome. This is fine if you are both the same size but embarrassing if there is much difference. I once sustained such welcoming hugs from a portly gentleman who held onto me for rather longer - and tighter - than was really necessary.

The party continues after the bigwigs have left and the agility of the young boys is tested as they stand on each others shoulders in an endeavour to mount and balance on the walls surrounding the arena. Spreading their arms and concentrating on the horizon they make ready for the death defying act of seeing who can travel the quickest and furthest before falling off........and possibly breaking a few bones! Scallywags, now devoid of school uniforms and footwear, run alongside the wall shouting all manner of abuse at Houdinis, hoping to put them off balance as they near certain obstacles. Several places en route have crumbling stonework and gaps but with bare feet and wavering arms ready to take flight if the attempt at the world record fails, their hesitation is momentary as they effect a perfect hurdle - much to the disappointment of the crowd below. I understand no one has ever completed the whole course but several broken bones have been sustained and these are displayed as a soldier would wear his distinguished war medals.

At the back of the stadium a small group of young boys enter a peeing competition. They stand in line and take it in turn to see who can pee the furthest. A stone is placed immediately in the exact spot when each individual pee has reached its furthest point. Judging is strict and scuffles often break out when disagreements ensue which means the competition has to begin all over again, this raises the question of how a continual flow can be sustained. I don't think the winner gets a prize but am certain his standing within the team ascends several notches! These groups are also adept at disappearing extremely quickly should anyone decide to take the back way out of the stadium.

A complicated game of jack stones is another pastime played by both boys and girls and several groups can always be found competing throughout the day. Adults and children also play a phenomenally speedy game of draughts with green and red bottle tops and a marked out square of rough wood. A game often moves so quickly it is difficult to follow and is over in a matter of minutes, hands shaken and the next game launched.

The older girls and boys use the day as a free dating agency. They all wander nonchalantly around for a time pretending they are not interested in one another, the boys sauntering after the girls. Then the girls, in their very best dresses, turn and pass quick coy glances at the boys; the smiling boys place a well scrubbed hand over their mouths as they make a comment to their comrades; the girls giggle and so progress is made and conversations finally ensue. That is until towards evening when anxious parents will gather their brood together and the dating agency must wait for another event if further introductions are to be made.

Many town shops will open in the evening and one can purchase roast potatoes and corn cobs, trinkets and bonbons from the side stalls if one has the necessary francs. Many families have to be content with enjoying just the aromas and company of friends, but it can be a pleasurable time for catching up with gossip and relations who, perhaps, are able to come to town but once a year.

Hero's Day is a day when those who were involved in, lost loved ones or remember the genocide and ensuing war, no doubt hail as heroes those who fought for peace.

There are many heroes in today's Rwanda who strive to annihilate poverty and disease and work towards a classless and tolerant form of society where people will have the freedom of speech, enough food and clean water to put on their table and the threat of further conflict extinguished for ever.

Chapter Nine

'A true companion is loving all the time
and is a brother that is born for when there is distress'
                                        Proverbs 18:17

Kaz in Uganda

Kaz stood up and walked a short distance from the reclining group. Turning round abruptly he asked, 'Why don't we desert and make our way over the border, we could try to find your uncle and see if he will help us, our lives couldn't be any worse than they are now?'

Gasps of astonishment and questions as to the credibility of such a scheme tumbled out but no one said they were not prepared to participate. The dangers were formidable; lack of food; distance to travel; no one was sure how far it was to Kisoro or even the Ugandan border, but it was decided unanimously to go regardless of the many risks.

Fortunately Kaz and Robert, after their time with the army, had considerable knowledge of tracking and following the sun during the day so there would be no difficulty in moving east towards their ultimate goal - Uganda!

Most of what was left of their apologies for uniforms was either turned inside out or discarded to avoid detection as soldiers. Various objects found en route were quickly put to good use. A piece of blown out tyre was expertly shaped to fit inside a pair of boots whose soles were more holey than righteous. The bleeding inhabitants of these particular boots were in such a shocking condition they were bound with the remains of a shredded army jacket before being painfully eased into the repaired 'footwear.'

They dug for roots, which were eaten raw, and Kaz put into practice the lessons taught him by the pygmies. Having to keep on the move they were unable to set traps but any dead animals were skinned and eaten raw despite the persistent flies competing with this necessary source of protein.

Nights in the mountains proved cold and their hunger pains were almost unbearable but the fatigued little group pressed forward and stayed under cover as much as possible prostrating themselves immediately at the slightest sound. Branches were gathered and laid primate fashion for bedding and sleeping positions changed regularly during the night to distribute body warmth.

On waking before dawn one morning they were unable to arouse Bunani, the youngest of the group. He was stiff and cold. He was dead.

No one spoke for several minutes then they looked at one another and wondered who would be next. Robert raised a grimy, trembling hand and gently closed Bunani's staring eyes, as he had many others before, then slowly he buttoned the tattered jacket preparing Bunani for his long, last journey he knew not where.

After reverently placing Bunani in the undergrowth they recited the few solemn words of prayer any of them could remember, gathered their sparse belongings together and headed east once more. There were tears but no looking back.

Robert brought the exhausted group to a halt and asked if anyone could hear water flowing. Moving ever nearer to the gushing sound they thought they had found the Congo River, the river they had crossed when with the battalion which was now heading towards Kinshasha; Kisangani would be the next major town the boys would need to avoid.

Their gaunt, filthy frames were continually prostrated on the forest floor in their endeavours to avoid capture and, as they had no papers or passports it was decided when, and if, they neared Kisoro, Robert would attempt to find his relatives while the others stayed hidden.

It had been seven or eight years since he had stayed with his uncle, the area had altered; Robert couldn't remember the exact whereabouts of his relative's farm for previous visits had been through Cyanika then over the Rwandan/Ugandan border.

His straggly, filthy, long hair and emaciated body hadn't been washed for many months with the consequence no one would talk to him until finally an elderly lady, bent nearly double, took pity on Robert and hobbled along with him pointing out a track between a field of sorghum which she thought belonged to his uncle.

Within five minutes he recognised the farmhouse and tentatively approached the closed door and with a shaking hand knocked gently. It was opened by a buxom, kindly looking woman whom Robert recognised immediately as his aunt. She was older, but definitely the one who had shown such kindness to him and his family. She didn't recognise Robert and backed into the house, but Robert moved forward putting his foot in the door preventing her from closing it. 'What do you want?' she shouted as she desperately tried to stop him entering the room.

'I'm your nephew Robert, remember our family stayed with you many times in the past?' He repeated his name again and again, and that of his father, but still the aunt wasn't sure for he was unrecognisable as the nephew she had once known.

Robert answered several other pertinent questions in an endeavour to prove his identity and was finally welcomed inside. A message was sent to his uncle working in the fields while Robert was taken to wash his hands and given food and water. He tried desperately not to gulp everything down but, not having eaten any proper food for months, this wasn't easy - he was ravenous.

The reunion of nephew and uncle was tearful for no news of the family had been received for many years and the terrible condition of their nephew was distressing.

Robert wasn't sure how he should approach the subject of the other boys but, after relating a resume of his life over the last few years and the fact that his friends were in hiding just a short distance away, Robert and his uncle were soon on their way to collect them.

Initially the boys were dubious about coming out of hiding, for Robert had been absent for several hours, but once they saw Robert had a big smile on his face and maize cobs in his hands resistance disappeared and all made their way to the farmhouse hungrily eating the cobs as they walked.

Heads were shaved, bodies washed in **warm** water with real soap and a farm hand was sent to the local market where second hand shorts and tops were purchased. Beautiful soft clean blankets were shared between them for sleeping.

A limited amount of food was eaten initially to avoid sickness and diarrhoea, and on their first night of freedom they were afraid to close their tired, red eyes for fear this unbelievable dream would disappear. They talked well into the night until one by one a wonderful relaxed slumber visited them all.

The uncle was unable to foster all the boys so Robert stayed with his relatives and foster homes were found for Kaz and the other boys. They all returned to school and Kaz acted as houseboy to his foster parents when not at school. He worked hard and obtained a reasonable level in several subjects. His foster father also taught him to till the ground, grow potatoes and maize and how to milk and tend the family's two cows.

There were four other children in the family who were aware of Kaz's horrific childhood so treated him kindly enough but it was not the same as having his own Rwandan family.

Unfortunately, Kaz's foster father died of AIDS and Kaz, at the age of fourteen, left school to help look after his foster mother and the farm until the year 2001 when she also died.

As 'peace' was imminent in Rwanda Kaz decided to try to return to his mother country so visited the Ugandan embassy in Kampala for advice. There was no problem in him returning to Rwanda but was given only travel money arriving in Ruhengeri with very little money, no relatives, no future, no life.

As we will see in a later chapter Kaz was not the only one left without relatives and the possibility of a life of poverty.

Chapter Ten

'What we know, or what we believe,
is in the end of little consequence'.
'The only consequence is what we do.'

John Ruskin

Sick Baby and White Dove

I will always remember the day I thought an emaciated, illegitimate baby was going to die. An unmarried mother had left the child with its grandmother and disappeared.

As I wandered through the airless village early one morning greeting women as they prepared for their day's work, a runny nosed but bright eyed boy, of about four year's of age, took my hand and led me to a mud and sand, windowless hut. Before entering the dim, foul smelling room I called out but there was no response. The sunlight from the open door revealed a bundle of rags in the corner underneath which I found a little body. The thin, black face I recognised as the baby I'd seen on several occasions as I passed through the village on my way to work. The child always sat with bare bottom on bare earth, crying as it stared at the other children playing.

The bundle was cold and lifeless but I found a weak pulse so took the baby with me to the compound because no one knew the grandmother's whereabouts. The local women thought she was working in the fields.

The child, a girl, was lying in a pool of obnoxious smelling diarrhoea so I needed to discard her rags and wash her body before deciding upon further action.

Luckily the sun had warmed the water in my plastic container so I bathed the child and wrapped it in a clean towel. Her spindly arms and legs and distended stomach spoke of malnutrition and she was dehydrated from chronic diarrhoea. The first teaspoonful of boiled water I gave her dribbled from her mouth, as did the second half-an-hour later, but on the sixth attempt the water disappeared.

The grandmother returned in the late afternoon but made no effort to find me, although I'm sure she knew I had the baby, so I found her and asked if the baby could be taken to hospital. This suggestion was refused.

The child was returned to the grandmother for the night with clean clothes, a napkin made from one of my towels and strict instructions that nothing but boiled water, which I provided in a flask, was to be administered from my clean cup and spoon.

The young boy arrived again early the next morning, with the child, and I made him understand he must stay with her while I tried to get a lift on the back of bicycle and visit a chemist in Ruhengeri.

On reaching the main road the bicycle taxis circled me like hungry sharks but, on finally making my choice, I was soon on my way to town. There I found a pharmacy, run by an Asian, whose shelves seemed sadly depleted for they displayed only one or two packets and bottles for sale.

Luckily the Asian spoke a little English so I was able to ask for a chronic diarrhoea remedy and perhaps some dried milk. The remedy was no problem but would be expensive and there was a negative shake of the head when I again requested dried milk.

Having paid for the medicine I was about to leave when the Asian raised a finger and told me to wait. He disappeared into the back of the shop and, after several minutes, reappeared blowing the dust from a packet of special dried soya milk dated 1998 which had pictured on the front of the box a laughing, robust white child with podgy arms and legs. Below the instructions it stated the contents were good for building strong healthy babies! Stashed in my own store I had eggs, which a kindly farmer had brought me for the clothes I had left with his family, also bananas, rice and a few arrowroot biscuits from England, these items I felt would also help the baby's recovery.

The child obviously needed medical attention and a drip but the grandmother again refused a hospital visit even though I offered to pay the fee. All I could do was to keep the child clean, warm and infused with a constant flow of liquid and hope a spark of new life would soon return to the little being.

The second day was harrowing for the diarrhoea still persisted, as did the negativity of the grandmother. She had previously been trying to feed the baby boiled potatoes and 'farty' beans with very little liquid. This is the diet of the poor.

I washed and changed the baby the following morning and gave her sips of boiled water throughout the day. Towards evening the boiled water was exchanged for a very mild concoction of the 1998 baby soya milk and I prayed this little girl would maybe, one day, look as robust and healthy as the baby on the front of the soya milk packet. I continued this fortified liquid diet for a further two days and on the third day crumbled arrowroot biscuit into the milk. When the diarrhoea had almost cleared, mashed banana and maize porridge completed the menu until I was able to introduce vegetables, eggs, rice and any other strength building food I could obtain.

During this time I also treated the child's badly infected index finger on the right hand for somehow, I never did find out why, an elastic band had been wound tightly around the base of the finger impeding the blood flow. It resembled a liver sausage, the flesh having gone black. Luckily I must have released the elastic band in time for the blood to flow but it took several weeks before a new skin began to form and satisfactory healing take place.

Every night I returned the baby to its grandmother and, although still lethargic her eyes were wide open and reasonably clear and she was beginning to enjoy the daily variety of food. The grandmother said the baby only had to hear my voice and she would turn her head waiting for me to appear. When I did materialize her little face lit up and spindly little arms reached out.

Tears filled my eyes each time I held that baby girl as she snuggled into my arms. More than once I thought seriously about trying to take her back to the UK with me for I had no way of knowing what would happen to her once I left. I had to be satisfied with the fact that I knew the child would now live – or should I say exist – but for how long?

It was during this worrying, but memorable episode a white dove appeared in the cupped hands of two village boys. They said they had found it being attacked by a red kite. Its heart was racing and it had a long piece of string tied to one of its legs and several feathers sticking out at unorthodox angles. I took the bird from them and examined its wings and body and could see no serious injuries. The boys, I think, had brought it as a present for me but I explained I didn't agree with caged animals and it must be released.

We scattered biscuit crumbs and grains of rice before releasing the dove but it made no attempt to eat or fly immediately, instead it nestled on the ground. We sat watching for some time as darkness descended and a full moon slowly edged its way into the night sky. Suddenly the dove flapped its wings and managed a laboured flight to the roof. It was on the ground the next morning and I thought perhaps a raptor had attacked it, but as I walked forward it flew onto my roof with ease. The food scattered overnight had disappeared but I was not sure whether the dove had feasted or my friends the rats had been visiting again.

That evening, when I returned from work on the pipeline, the dove was walking backwards and forwards along the roof and, to my delight, it finally flew to the food I threw down. The children from the village were, by that time, enthralled with this white spectre and the fact that it actually came within inches of my feet, its bobbing head pecking, eyeing me, and then pecking again. I had to encourage the children not to frighten it for the few wild creatures that now inhabit Rwanda are usually edible and, therefore, fair game!

Before long it had become remarkably tame and would fly down for its food whenever I was about, and sleep under the eaves of a thatch overnight. Many in the village thought I had magic qualities, which I found extremely disturbing. I tried to dispel such notions and, although I became very fond of the creature, I was really pleased when it decided to leave. I was not sure if it left of its own volition or whether the red kite had paid a visit. There were no white feathers scattered around so prayed it was the former. My white dove had survived as had my baby.

Another day I will always remember. On returning to visit the village seven months later I immediately enquired about the health of my baby. When told the grandmother had disappeared my heart sank. Fortunately, I found a mother, with six children of her own, nursing my baby girl. I was unable to stem the flow of tears when, on hearing my voice, the child held out her arms and anchored them around my neck as I took her from the dear, caring mother. The child's grandmother had left the village one morning shouldering her hoe and never returned. Each day this mother walked several kilometres to work in the fields taking my baby and her youngest children with her. The Trust made sure that food was taken to this family at regular intervals and this child is now a member of a loving family.

Chapter Eleven

'In the wilderness I sense the miracle of life
and behind it our scientific accomplishments fade to trivia'
Charles A. Lindbergh

Walk on the Wild Side

It had mercifully rained heavily just before dawn, and everyone was out collecting water before it gradually soaked into the parched earth. Several children were using rusty tins to scoop up the clay coloured dregs from puddles that would soon disappear once the sun materialised.

Several of our many generous sponsors in the UK had requested their donations be spent on water projects and the three kilometre pipeline, beginning near the pumping station built by the World Bank at the base of Karisimbe, was nearing completion; crystal clear water would soon be wending its way from a spring on the mountain to Mgwati and Musekera, two villages in the foothills of the Virunga mountains.

There were no mechanical diggers or morning and afternoon tea breaks, only the rhythmic swinging of heavy, long handled hoes as the men and women cut into the dehydrated earth for eight long hours each day, resting for thirty minutes when the sun was at its height.

It was nearing four o'clock when these stout hoes were hoisted onto even stouter shoulders. I trudged wearily to the market place and sat on the baked earth with an aching back propped up against an undulating wall of sandstone and mud waiting, with what seemed like the entire population of Kinigi, for the bus to Ruhengeri twelve kilometres away. There I would alight and walk the rest of the way to my base at Imbaraga village.

By 4.30pm the bus had not arrived so a ten kilometre cross country walk loomed and the inevitable descent of nightfall at 6.30pm. With a two litre empty water bottle, hair thick with dust and a body streaked with sweat, I set off at the rhythmic pace I'd learned to trust. It rarely faltered and there had been very few Rwandans prepared to accompany me on such a trek. It wasn't a fast pace but I kept each stride about the same length and each second produced about two equal strides. I can keep this pace up all day once my brain has acclimatized to the fact that there are many kilometres to complete, so any travelling companions are soon left behind.

Many villagers had never seen a white woman especially one on her own, walking in the foothills of the Virungas, dressed in old, mud splattered boots and trousers and a floppy, faded sun hat.

Wherever I walked I encountered small groups, mainly children, en route who sometimes wanted to walk with me for a short distance or pointed and giggled then ran off and hid from the Mzungu. I always kept a few bonbons in my knee pocket purposely to make friends with them. Unfortunately these enticements generally became a sticky blob adhering to the transparent paper after spending time in ninety degrees for most of the day but were still accepted, with great delight, by both old and young.

After about half an hour I came across five thatched huts framed by a few banana trees which provided shade for several women dressed in brightly coloured gukenyeras (wrap around pieces of material). Children, meticulously sorting through stones ready for their game of jackstones, immediately ran for shelter as I stepped into view. Even the women backed away until I stopped and greeted them with a broad smile and in Kinyarwanda said, 'Muraho, amakuru?' A young woman with a baby in her arms approached and returned my greeting, 'Ni meza.' Unfortunately her baby took one look at the Mzungu, closed its eyes, screwed up its little face until it resembled a dried prune then let out an unearthly scream. It then took a quick gulp of air, held its breath for an excruciatingly length of time, before emitting another piercing shriek. The heads of other children, who had been hiding behind huts or tree trunks, popped out as though on cue as in a stage musical, the baby providing the theme music. By this time the adults wanted to engage in conversation so I turned my white face away from the baby and waited while the mother soothed and stroked the baby's back as it endeavoured to dig its way into her neck. Luckily I still had a few sticky bonbons and these soon enticed the children from their hiding places, including the baby, and after a brief chat with the women, mostly in sign language, I continued my journey.

I had walked for some considerable time into the setting sun when

I heard rasping noises and couldn't resist bearing left through a small maize field to discover the cause. I was amazed to find several men whose feet seemingly hovered above a deep ravine. They bent from the waist and moved up and down like yo-yo's.

A rough track bordered the field and, alongside it, sturdy planks of sawn wood were placed at intervals across this deep gorge. Whole denuded trees, balanced across these planks, were being cut. There were eight men working in twos, one of the partnership was in the bottom of the ravine holding the end of a six foot long, savage looking, tapered saw with shark like teeth, another man was balanced precariously above, astride the tree trunk, as he grasped the saw's other handle. Both men synchronized their actions perfectly as they pushed and pulled up and down, up and down. The rhythm was only interrupted when the tree had to be moved forward and again secured with large cheese-like wedges. Planks were cut from these massive trees as straight as any western mechanical machine could have cut them.

These men had been working from seven o'clock in the morning without so much as a drink of water. The man in the bottom of the gorge was stripped to the waist, his black body glistening with sweat which ran down his acutely visible rib cage; he wore a hat made from plaited banana leaves and sawdust coated his face and shoulders as he stood calf-deep in wood shavings. The bare foot man above him also had a hat of dried leaves and wore a T-shirt and knee length trousers that were barely respectable. They waved to me so I walked over to talk apologizing for having no water to give them but promised to leave a couple of bottles the next day in a prearranged niche - if I had to walk again!

The following morning the bus didn't arrive so I walked again to the site where we were digging trenches for the pipeline En route the 'Saw Men' were already at work and grateful I had remembered their bottles of water. There seemed to be a pecking order, those on the upper deck always drank first and often there was little water left for the men below. This was something I never questioned!

What I did question was the treatment of some of the mentally ill one of whom I met on my journey that morning.

Nearing a village on the way to Kinigi I noticed a tall, Lowry stick-man man shuffling towards me. He wore a broad brimmed black hat, a torn, dirty long coat, trousers and over-sized scruffy boots. His face was gaunt, his eyes dull and lifeless and from around his ankles a chain extended up and around his wrists resembling those you see prisoners wearing on death row when exercising. The shackles restricted his movements and he could only move one foot forward a few inches in front of the other as he shuffled along. As he passed me the stench was overpowering and I noticed his hands were bloodied presumably from rubbing on the chains. I walked for a few minutes before turning round to look at him. He had squatted on a large stone and, although people were passing, no-one took any notice of him.

Sometime later I asked my friend, the nurse in Ruhengeri, why this man was in chains and was informed he was mentally ill and restricted in this way to prevent him harming anyone! I made several diplomatic enquiries to see if I could do anything for this poor soul but was told, 'There is no institution available for such people and at least he has a certain amount of freedom.'

The lack of doctors, hospitals and treatment in the outlying districts proved a constant problem and there were many occasions when it was necessary to refer to my book 'Where There is No Doctor' in an endeavour to treat minor ailments and injuries. Although, on arriving 'home' on this particular day, the brandy flask also came in very handy.

Several children came running towards me pointing to a little boy with a severe gash on the side of his leg. The blood flowed freely which was a good thing for it helped to clean the wound - a wound that needed stitching; we were miles from any hospital.

Before making a fire I bandaged the leg to stem the flow but soon found the bandages were soaked through. On further inspection I decided the embroidery lessons, taught me by my grandmother, would need to be put into practice. A length of nylon cotton was immersed in boiling water and a curved needle, found in my first aid kit, was dipped into a little brandy; the boy I gave a quarter cup full which I told him to knock straight back. This brought tears to his eyes but not a sound of contention apart from a couple of gasping coughs - and so the operation should have commenced. Unfortunately I chickened out at the last minute and stood hovering with needle poised. Eyeing the brandy flask I resolved it would not do me any harm to take a slug - and then another - and so the wound was stitched! Four years later there is a very neat four centimetre scar of which my patient is very proud - so am I!

Chapter Twelve

'Seeing in not sufficient, you have to be able to feel then act'

Emmanuel, John and Others Needing Help

October in the UK usually finds me with an ailment best known as itchy feet; it's time to return to Rwanda. I look forward to completing new projects, returning our orphans to their studies, making new friends and renewing old acquaintances. Unfortunately, there is always a flip side to these journeys and inevitably the seasons have taken their toll. Each time I return someone I know has died either from malaria, TB, AIDS, malnutrition or just from being unable to cope anymore, Emmanuel was such a boy.

I found him curled in a foetal position outside a hovel in the village of Urugaga. I thought he was dead for there was no movement as I stood beside him. Apart from a little of his face the top half of his body was completely covered in a filthy nylon greyish anorak. The sleeves extended over his hands and what was left of the hood was pulled over his head. A pair of dirty, ragged trousers covered the remainder of his body, his feet were bare.

On kneeling down two blood-shot eyes flickered open, slowly at first then, wide and blinking. He raised himself into a sitting position and for the next five minutes a hacking cough racked his emaciated body. I made no attempt to help but asked if there was anything I could do. I could speak very little Kinyarwanda but I think he understood for he nodded, struggled to his feet and indicated I should follow him into the hovel.

His home was circular, about eight feet in diameter, and constructed of rough volcanic stone. The conical roof was partially covered in old tarpaulins, coats and bits of tin most of which let in daylight and, no doubt, rain. The inside area was separated into two sections and furnished with old clothing and dried branches. On the dried mud floor lay a ragged rush mat, this I presumed was his sleeping quarters. Three blackened, various sized, dented pots stood in another corner together with a bunch of kindling sticks. It all oozed poverty and deprivation.

We sat on the stinking mat for a while and he permitted me to pull back his hood revealing a head and hands covered in sores. At first I felt revulsion but realised I must do something for this poor boy; I was in Rwanda to help its people and here was someone who certainly needed help.

Emmanuel was in no condition to walk to the nearest hospital and there was no doctor we could call or visit. I managed to get a man with a motor bike to take us (yes, three of us on a motorbike!) to the hospital where I paid for the boy's examination.

He was stripped, turned round several times then his throat and chest examined. I was horrified to note his body was emaciated and a mass of sores. He was told to dress and I was given a prescription for antibiotics, several other tablets and Dettol soap with instructions to ensure he washed daily and took his medication regularly.

Water for bathing was a problem but our daily ritual consisted of half filling my bowl with water, Emmanuel then stood in the bowl and washed from top to toe with the antiseptic Dettol soap. I turned away and waited while he washed the lower part of his body, which was covered with a pair of girl's knickers, and when he'd finished I washed his legs and feet. I found him a clean pair of long trousers, a T-shirt and my navy blue sweat shirt sporting a hood, these he wore while I washed and repaired his clothing.

I was reluctant to administer my cough mixture and vitamins until he had completed his course of tablets, and was initially careful with both food and medication because he could digest only liquids for a while, diarrhoea being prevalent. Eventually quality food, such as rice, bananas and vegetables, was included in his diet.

I visited his den three times a day to administer the tablets and within ten days found him wandering towards me, and sometimes watching from a distance when I was teaching or playing games with the children. He never joined in, I don't think he had the strength, but I was thrilled to find he slowly improved and many of the sores ceased suppurating and the cough eased.

I thought he was about nine years old but later found he was seventeen!

Before I returned for the UK I left money to pay for another visit to the hospital if his health deteriorated, plus a sack of rice, dried fish, maize, vitamins, Dettol soap and the promise I would return in seven month's time.

I returned to find he was buried under a small pile of volcanic stones four metres from his hovel home. There was no-one to afford him a proper burial, as is the case with so many deaths in Africa, but his memory lives on. The Trust built a children's dwelling and this has a name plaque over the door - 'Maison Emmanuel.'

Fortunately, there are success stories. John, a tall thin boy of about eighteen, had been seriously ill with TB, and although much improved after twelve months treatment, he had to give up the work with his rented bicycle on which he carried pillion passengers and goods for a living. He was unable to continue with any heavy duties but the local authorities agreed to allocate him a free space in Ruhengeri market for twelve months and I managed to purchase a second-hand, but very serviceable, treadle machine for repairing leather. He is now self employed, has retained his self respect and supplies his twin sister and her disabled three year old son, Elie, with a weekly supply of essential food such as rice, eggs, esombe and sometimes a little dried fish.

The Trust managed to obtain an appointment for Elie to see a doctor in the southern province and now, after several visits, Elie is wearing calipers in the hopes they will improve his problem legs.

Fourteen year old Francois was unable to continue his studies because he could no longer see the blackboard or read print clearly. We managed to get him to hospital for an eye test and subsequent small operation. He now wears glasses and has recently gained his first Engineering Diploma.

An amusing success story is of a man who visited me one night bent double in severe pain. He shuffled slowly towards my fire issuing throaty groans while rubbing his distended stomach.

His attire consisted of what had once been a blue T- shirt, fraying calf-length trousers, no shoes and a few black teeth; neither of us spoke as I pressed the appendix area. I knew if the pain was acute I was in no position to perform an appendectomy for, even though my medical kit was extensive by Rwandan standards, I didn't think my Swiss army knife and 'Where There is no Doctor' manual would suffice. Plus the fact the brandy flask was sadly depleted.

'Oya' ('No') it didn't hurt when I kneaded the appendix area several times so brought my hand to the stomach region and discovered a vine had been tied tightly around his middle, directly under the rib cage. This is a solution adapted for many torso pains; a vine tied above or below the afflicted area prevents pain from travelling farther up or down. Or so they say!

I cut the 'trap' which had left a bright red indentation and investigated his bloated stomach. The usual diet of potatoes, and what I term 'farty' beans, is not conducive to healthy innards or digestion and extremely strong smelling, explosive wind is something I have to contend with from adults and especially children. I decided a good dose of anti-indigestion Peptac might help any digestive problems he may have and, even if it didn't it wouldn't do the poor man any harm. He took the slightly glutinous, pink, peppermint tasting liquid, drank it without hesitation then sat quietly contemplating.

Eventually he decided the medicine had not had the desired affect so, still bent and groaning a little, he gathered a few dried leaves, rolled them into a cigar shape, pushed them into his rear end and moved jerkily around in a circle issuing spasmodic, guttural grunts which reminded me of a slow motion tribal war dance. It finally struck me just what the problem might be – constipation!

Fortunately my comprehensive medical kit included Sennacots so I prescribed two tablets and pretended to put them into my mouth and drink from a cup. I then placed the tablets in his grubby hand, put my hands together under my chin, inclined my head a little to the right, closed my eyes and professed to sleep. He nodded, shook my hands vigorously with several 'Muracoze cane' (thank you very much) and disappeared into the night, still groaning, rubbing his middle region and clutching the prescribed tablets.

Many of my instructions were in sign language for they had fast become a solution to my lack of Kinyarwanda and were most useful when teaching children who picked up this form of teaching very quickly - and thought it fun.

About the same time the following evening my patient appeared, upright, arms extended and thumbs pointed upwards, a broad grin on his near toothless, black face. From his pocket he produced a maize cob, which he ceremoniously placed at my feet, after which he kissed the palms of both of my hands and with a jaunty turn disappeared into the forest. I presumed my diagnoses had been correct!

Chapter Thirteen

*'As long as we fail to address the issue of the world's population
explosion everything we do in an attempt to save this planet will
prove cosmetic and trivial. We may initially win the battle to save
the giant panda but lose the war of the world. It's commonsense,
this continuous human mushrooming will swamp everything'*

DJR

Birth Control, Family Planning and AIDS

During my visits to Rwanda I became abundantly aware that no
amount of aid, consisting of finance, water or food would solve
the poverty situation if the women were continually reduced to
producing such large families and no attempt made to eradicate
AIDS. There was also an obvious need for protection during sex
and urgent research into a cure for HIV and AIDS.

I was in an unstable foreign country and had to tread cautiously
if our Trust was ever to pioneer a family planning programme.

Late one evening a heavily pregnant woman arrived at my hut
with a sleeping child strapped to her back. She had nine other
children. Many people think third world women are unable to
experience the same feelings as their contemporaries in the west -
I can assure them they can. This woman was suicidal!

Chantelle was 35 years of age but looked 50. She spoke halting
French and I managed to explain I could do nothing further to help
her until after the birth of her baby and before she had discussed
any of my suggestions with her husband.

Was this the answer to my prayers and a possible way of
introducing an alien, but most necessary programme to the wilds of
a foreign country?

I also explained I had a Rwandan friend whom I felt she should
meet; Dorothea, a retired midwife/nurse was prepared to help me
with setting up a birth control project.

Dorothea met Chantelle two days later and it soon became obvious
Chantelle's knowledge regarding sex, birth control and AIDS
was negligible. The conversation began with basics and we
confirmed that further pregnancies could be prevented but she must

first obtain her husband's permission if she wanted to practise birth control; we didn't want to cause unnecessary problems in a home where the husband may indulge in wife beating.

Dorothea and I had a gut feeling we wouldn't see Chantelle again once she had tried to discuss the matter with her husband - if she discussed it at all! African men can be overtly macho regarding birth control and family planning. Intimacy of any kind, I found, was only discussed among the women and sex was a part of their lives to be endured not enjoyed.

To my utter amazement Chantelle returned a few nights later with her tired looking husband who agreed with our suggestions!

He told me, 'I love my wife but how can I love her without us having more children?' I assured him it was certainly possible and we could begin a few months after the baby was born if that was the method they chose. The expression on the couple's faces was a joy to be seen as they vehemently shook both my hands before leaving.

I don't suppose one would find many African men responding so positively, so quickly but I had and I was over the moon!

Within a week thirty two women had visited me and all wanted, 'the same as Chantelle' so our first meeting was arranged for a Sunday afternoon in the village where I was living. Dorothea and I were busy completing report forms as the ladies, attired in their Sunday best and accompanied by dozens of barefoot, noisy children, assembled around us.

A large square of wood painted black resembled a blackboard and, with my chalk from UK, Dorothea drew a woman's internal reproductive system explaining how a baby was conceived when impregnated with sperm. She also explained the several ways pregnancy could be avoided and the fact that family planning did not kill but was a method of prevention. Very few of the women truly realised what their internal organs looked like or how they worked.

I soon received many requests to visit outlying villages in the foothills of the Virungas so Dorothea and I spent our Sundays, often walking many kilometres, spreading the word about family planning to poor families in the Northern Province of Rwanda. Hence our birth control/family planning/AIDS programme was born and my prayers were answered.

There were several methods of birth control available, these included two and three monthly injections, implants lasting five years, the pill (not very satisfactory because the women forget to take it) condoms, and the natural method (also not always very satisfactory).

Our Trust was prepared to pay for women who were unable to afford the treatment and, over the next few years, the groups mushroomed to the extent I felt the government needed to be involved.

I kept records and, in due course, gave copies to the appropriate authorities. To my delight when I returned to Rwanda in 2010 free birth control was available to all women with a health card. This card cost 1,000 Rwandan francs (the equivalent of about £1.30) for twelve months and our Trust helped any woman unable to afford this - unbelievably, there were many.

There have, of course, been problems over the years. One woman from Muhabura came to our meeting in that area but I was informed, during subsequent meetings the following year, she had been severely beaten by her husband for attending. I decided the only way to deal with such a situation was to ask two of the men, whom I knew supported their wives in our programme, to go and speak with the wife beater and explain the advantages they had experienced by being part of this project. I will definitely be looking out for this woman when I return.

Chapter Fourteen

'But the child's sob in the silence courses deeper
than the strong man in his wrath'
Elizabeth Barrett Browning

Pascal K

Pascal K lay with his two elder brothers and younger sister on a rush mat which covered the earth floor of their family hut. Placide and Dancilla, their parents, sat at a roughly hewn wooden table on which the flame of a half-burnt candle stuttered as it lit the small, airless room casting undecipherable shadows on the mud walls. A flicker of light rested on the face of one child illuminating its large, dark chocolate pupils in lakes of opal, framed by long curling black lashes. These eyes were wide open. These eyes were filled with terror!

Quick footsteps approached the hut and Placide picked up a sturdy log from the corner of the room and stood with his back to the wall behind the rickety bamboo door. The door flew open with such force it extinguished the candle's flame plunging the room into darkness. Terrified by the intrusion, muffled whimpers could be heard from the children as they huddled together for protection.

'We must vacate the village immediately, the massacre has begun,' commanded an elder as he felt his way into the tar black room. 'Gather anything you can and go NOW!' He left as quickly as he arrived.

'G..g....go where?' was all Placide could stutter. They could hear gunfire and see the red glow of fires lighting up the horizon only a short distance away to the east.

After several attempts, and with trembling hands, Dancilla relit the candle and the family frantically gathered what little food and clothing they had in the hut and set off in the opposite direction to the gunfire.

'Stay close; keep in line; no talking; tap the shoulder in front if you need to make contact,' ordered Placide.

Pascal's young sister was carried on her father's lean shoulders as he blindly led his family through a parched maize field. Her thin little arms were clasped tightly around his forehead, her legs and feet jutted out from his shoulders as though pointing the way to safety.

Just a ragged half circle of moon was visible for threatening clouds had gathered over the Virunga mountains and promised much needed rain. A slight breeze stimulated gentle movement amongst the tall, spindly stems of maize the family had hoped to harvest once the rains revived their parched roots.

The frightened group moved quickly and silently.

Suddenly, Placide stopped and held up his hand, he was perplexed by a droning sound from above. The menacing, black outline of an aeroplane passed directly above them etched against the now full, grey moon. Instantly they fell to the ground; the young child pitched forward and cried out as she hit the earth a few feet in front of her father taking several maize plants down with her. Placide reached out and covered her with his body both as protection and to stifle her cries.

The hum of the plane's engine ebbed away towards the orange glow but the sound of gunfire drew closer. Placide, Dancilla and the children rose hesitantly and Irakiza, the young daughter, was hoisted back onto her father's shoulders and the perilous journey began again. Placide decided they should make for the sparsely inhabited foothills of the Virungas an area affording plenty of forest cover and soft resting places.

There was complete silence apart from the occasional crack of a twig or crunch of dried leaves underfoot. The children knew there was to be complete obedience to their farther's instructions.

They had walked only a short distance when muffled voices could be heard close by. Silently, Placide motioned to his wife to stop; the children collided with one another before coming to a halt. The maize stems parted and they were immediately surrounded by half a dozen Interahamwe, thugs recruited for President Habyarimana's MRDN party.

Pascal's family were moderate Hutus with Tutsi neighbours and friends and were in no doubt the Interahamwe would be well aware of this.

'Ha! What have we here?' shouted one of the mob as he brandished a blood stained machete in front of the family. 'Thinking of taking a holiday are you, well, we're here to help you on your way.'

The family was roughly pushed into a circle with their backs facing inwards. The thugs sauntered round looking them up and down, tickling their throats with differing implements of torture. Pascal's young sister whimpered so was slapped hard across the face by the nearest hoodlum. She cried out and was slapped even harder then seized from her father's arms.

Placide instinctively moved forward to retrieve her but a machete sliced between his top two vertebrae allowing his chin to flop forward onto his chest. The executioner stepped quickly away to avoid the fountain of blood which spurted into the air. Placide remained upright for the next few seconds; head lolling; sleeping standing up as the colour of his T-shirt quickly changed from pale blue to red before he fell forward arms splayed as though ready for crucifixion.

The young girl was thrown from one thug to another laughing when they dropped her; Dancilla fell to her knees sobbing with hands clasped in prayer. The two terrified elder boys were not sure whether to help their mother and father or run into the maize but crumpled to the ground as they tried to flee, several bullets penetrating their young bodies. This proved a merciful killing. Dancilla endured a ritual of rape and torture before her body was kicked into the maize field together with the body of her young daughter who had been thrown between the thugs and caught on the sharp blades of their machetes.

Pascal K was stretched out across his brothers, alive but soaked in their blood, waiting for the blows which would allow him to enter what he prayed would be a better world. Guffaws of laughter from the frenzied murderers echoed across the fields as one grabbed Pascal by the waistband of his trousers and hauled him to his feet.

'What shall we do with this one?' asked the leader.

Several horrifying suggestions were made but the final decision was to leave him 'armless' thus providing the thugs with a good joke to relate to their comrades later.

His thin right arm was placed on a log and chopped off above the elbow with a blow from a machete still covered in the blood from his murdered family.

There were no warm embraces as the souls of the family's hacked and tortured bodies transcended from this world to the next. Pascal couldn't bring back time; a second ticked and was gone forever.

Within a minute hell or ecstasy can be etched on one's memory for a lifetime or stubbed out in that first tick.

A cool breeze eased the throb in Pascal's arm as he lay staring into an ever increasing pool of blood, a despairing reflection manifesting itself in waves of pain and grief. Sobs emanated from a body that was experiencing hell's fifty ninth tick. The next second Pascal experienced a visceral awareness and gradually a rainbow of colours swam before his bloodshot eyes as he drifted to join his family.

The Interahamwe had annihilated a complete family in less than fifteen minutes and this wouldn't be the last shocking drama to be staged that night.

Chapter Fifteen

*'If you find it in your heart to care for someone else,
you will have succeeded'*

Pascal K with the Batwa

The ground was dry and even the lightest footfall seemed to send a cacophonous invitation to his enemies. The murderers had left him to die but Pascal was alive. He wanted to run; fly; disappear but leaves, branches and grasses, once his friend, thought otherwise, they crunched and snapped as he crawled away to hide leaving his beloved family in their last bloody resting place.

His throbbing arm felt no real pain only the occasional stab in unison with the pulsating explosions in his head. He took his T-shirt off, held one sleeve between his teeth and struggled to tie the torn garment tightly around what was left of his right arm, hoping to stem the flow of blood. Pascal knew there was no possibility of a doctor or anyone to help him.

He felt weak and light headed from shock and loss of blood as he flattened his gaunt, exhausted body against the dried out sticks and torn tarpaulin which surrounded the outside toilet a few metres from a mud hut. The toilet had no roof and volcanic rocks had been thrown into the hole in the ground to act as a soak away.

As Pascal stumbled into the cesspit he endeavoured to stifle his cries as his body and wounded arm hit the uneven, rocky floor. He lay for a while praying his adversaries would not return to an empty village but soon realised he would be severely exposed should someone look over the edge; there was nothing but a few bits of dried bracken with which to cover himself

He listened for any sound of the enemy before he stood and balanced on the uneven rocks, then lunged with one arm towards the rim of the pit, only to fall back in excruciating pain. He tried again by digging his toes into the stones and soil supporting the walls of the pit and, with his good arm, he grasped at roots and vegetation as a lever. After what seemed an eternity he managed to heave his exhausted body over the edge of the abyss leaving his legs dangling while he struggled to draw breath.

Pascal remembered nothing after scrambling out of the cesspit until he became aware of floating above the ground with a strong light flickering among tall trees, flashes of brilliance compelling him to close his eyes. He attempted to turn his head a little to the left and found it was close to another head which bobbed up and down harmoniously with his but, on trying to turn his body, an agonising pain shot through his shoulder and down his arm. He had been taught there would be no pain or tears in Heaven if one had led a good life on earth, so where was he - in hell?

Rwandan voices drifted past him as he bounced along but it was sometime before he finally realised he was still alive. Immediately he panicked as memories of his murdered family returned. He tried to get off the roughly made stretcher but was anchored by vines tied around his chest and legs. Although unable to raise his hands in prayer he closed his eyes and prayed he would die before his captors reached their destination.

After what seemed an eternity the stretcher was placed unceremoniously on the ground and the bonds anchoring his body released. Two short strong arms helped him to his feet and half-naked, thin, muscular men, much shorter than himself, escorted him to a shaded spot in a small clearing. He had been rescued by pygmies from a Batwa tribe.

They dressed the stump of his severed arm with leaves from the umutagara tree and covered his shaking body with the remains of his bloodstained T-shirt. One of the men supported him to a rush mat and a strong smelling concoction, in a roughly carved wooden bowl, was held to his lips. Afraid to refuse Pascal swallowed the green liquid.

Within minutes he was swimming again in Lake Bulera, near his home, but the water was blood red. The sun's rays, which radiated not from above but from beneath him, suddenly began to duplicate, each cloned sun attaching itself like a magnet to ropes dangling from his feet. Almost immediately these varying sized suns began to rotate and Pascal's body joined the merry-go-round which slowly gathered speed, sucking him into a whirlpool of descending darkness. His legs finally detached themselves from his body and floated past him before he was somersaulted into oblivion.

He had no idea how long he had slept but his body felt relaxed and it wasn't until he stretched his arms he realised half of the right arm was missing. Each time he closed his eyes his thoughts strayed from the amputation and he imagined the arm was still attached.

A tiny wizened old woman, whose flat bosoms hung almost to her waist, knelt beside a meal of cooked potatoes. Pascal managed to heave himself into a sitting position and the plate, woven from dried fronds, was placed on the floor beside him. The grandmother smiled showing her few remaining teeth, browned from chewing dried tobacco leaves; she stroked his cheek with a hand reminiscent of sepia parchment and nails gnarled with years of toil. 'You're safe with us boy, we will feed and heal you,' she said kindly.

After eating most of the potatoes Pascal felt strong enough to venture from his shade. The surroundings were familiar for his home had been in such a setting but included maize and sorghum instead of so many trees. Here the trees were dense and varied shelters had been woven from gathered branches.

In the clearing half naked female Batwa were cooking on an open wood fire and one woman was chopping wood with a machete the sight of which made Pascal's stomach lurch into his throat. Several small naked children reached into a dirty woven basket and stuffed the contents into their hungry little mouths before scampering off when their mothers waved their arms and scolded them. The men, Pascal was informed, were out hunting but there was no mention of where they had found him or how long he had been with them. He declined to ask too many questions being so relieved to be safe for at least a short time.

He watched the peaceful scene finding it hard to believe, only a short time before, he had witnessed the horrific massacre of his family. Immediately beads of sweat formed on his forehead and his body shook uncontrollably as the scene passed before him again and again in slow motion. He was given another potion and soon his nervous system was completely inactive and consciousness totally suspended.

He awoke to find a male Batwa dressing what remained of his arm. It had not been bathed but a mixture of what looked like beige speckled clay had been pressed onto the wound. Blood had seeped through this concoction and had congealed and until this dressing fell off Pascal could not imagine what the stump would resemble. Fresh leaves were again wrapped around the wound and thin young vines wound neatly over the leaves creating a tribal arm band.

After a few days a young Twa girl tended the dressings and gradually Pascal's strength returned as did his nightmares. A mild repeat prescription was enlisted because he could rarely close his eyes without seeing his little sister dangling from the point of a machete or his father's head lolling on his still warm body.

The male Batwa's latest hunting expedition produced branches of esombe whose leaves were pounded ready for cooking then served with boiled potatoes stolen from a vacated patch in the foothills of Kinigi. A small monkey and three rodents, caught that day, were roasted on a stick over the open fire. Pascal was also introduced to grubs and insects as an important part of the Twa's diet but water was almost non-existent unless it rained then every container and waterproof piece of material was put into service.

Before the relentless sun coursed through the sky each morning, the Twa and Pascal sucked dew from plants and trees for this would probably be the only water they would find during that day. He was also able to help gather wood for the fire and amuse the children.

A young Twa girl, about Pascal's age, consoled him whenever his vivid nightmares returned. Sometimes he awoke bathed in perspiration to find the young girl lying beside him, she had heard his ramblings and heartrending cries and would stay with him until he was calm and sleeping once again.

He had seen his mother and father, and now the Twa lying together and no one took any notice. The closeness of the girl gave him comfort and her tenderness towards him eased his troubled nights.

Batwa hunters from another area brought news one evening that Paul Kagame's FPR were gaining ground and the Hutu Interahamwe were searching for, and eliminating, as many Tutsi and moderate Hutus as possible before they retreated. Pascal was to be moved and safely hidden.

Chapter Sixteen

War may sometimes be a necessary evil.
But no matter how necessary, it is always an evil, never good.
We will not learn how to live together in peace
by killing each other's children.

Jimmy Carter

Goodbye to Pascal K

The Batwa knew they must move Pascal K quickly and silently; being a volcanic region there were many areas one person could be hidden during the day. The Batwa girl gave Pascal K a small rush mat which she tucked under his arm and, accompanied by two of the Twa men, he was taken to a natural hiding place about a kilometre away from their present camp.

Pascal K had only what he stood up in and no food. The next few days passed extremely slowly the monotony relieved only when he was able to return to the Batwa at dusk and the thugs had spent their lust for killing. Occasionally he ventured cautiously a few steps from his 'cave' during the day but at the slightest sound he bolted, like a frightened animal, to what he hoped was invisibility and safety.

On returning to camp one night he was told the Interahamwe had been but had left without any suspicion of him having been sheltered there. The children had been warned, on pain of a beating, 'Nothing must be said about the boy if any strangers enter the camp.'

The young girl attended to the dressing on his arm which was beginning to heal, it resembled a multi coloured, undulating, wizened mound but he found he was managing to use it for holding and carrying.

Gunfire echoed through the mountains during the day and several times bombs dropped close to his hideout in the vicinity of the Virunga foothills. News came through that Kagame's FPR rebel forces were advancing. For days he was holed-up for fourteen long hours at a time as the fierce fighting continued, and sometimes he found his limbs were so cramped he needed to crawl for a short distance, when emerging at night, before being able to stand. Government Hutu forces were making their last desperate stand for

Kagame's incursions were proving rapid and successful.

Instead of the Batwa escorting Pascal K it was decided he should make his own way to their camp at night. He crawled out of his dark hiding place early one evening, listened, and surveyed the area carefully before beginning his trek to the Batwa camp. It was a heavily wooded area strewn with volcanic rocks and within minutes he was conscious of twigs snapping and muffled voices. He stopped and fell to the ground.

'Ah! We thought we'd heard movement when in this area a couple of days ago and here's the culprit,' said one of the captors.

Although there was no question of him being anything but a Hutu, they saw his arm had been severed and demanded to know where the remainder of his family were. Pascal K was tongue-tied with fright so, without hesitation, he was pushed to his knees and a heavy hoe produced with which to execute him.

His mind went blank and his body rigid as he waited for the fatal blow to the back of his head. One thug gripped his shoulder and held him down while the other stood a little distance behind him with the hoe ready poised to swing a blow that would smash his skull. Suddenly voices were heard and the executioner lowered the hoe and greeted a group of militia scouting the area for Tutsis.

Pascal remained paralysed, head bowed, until one of the militia pulled Pascal's head back and scrutinised his face.

'I know you don't I?' barked the man.

Pascal was still numb with terror and, although he didn't recognise the soldier, he nodded his head and prayed.

'Let the poor little sod go, I know his uncle. Can't you see he's Hutu and only a youngster? We'll have need of him one day.'

'Why's he missing an arm then?' asked the man with the hoe.

'How the hell should I know, ask him?' was the reply.

Pascal K was asked to explain how he'd lost his arm but his words were so garbled it was decided to let him go. The hoe was hoisted over the shoulder of the would-be executioner and Pascal fell forward onto his face not daring to move. There was raucous laughter as the men walked away leaving him in a sweating, pulsating, helpless heap.

Night was approaching and he was afraid of trying to find the Batwa for fear of incriminating them. Exhaustion enveloped every sinew and muscle as he levered himself onto his knees and crawled a few yards before trying to stand. His legs wouldn't support him and collapsing completely he lay down, curled up into a foetal ball and cried.

A myriad of stars slowly materialised in the heavens and Pascal prayed his family might be somewhere up there experiencing no more pain; no more hunger or thirst; no more suffering. Sheer fatigue allowed him but a few hours fitful sleep before dawn and the warm welcoming sun appeared, then hunger, thirst and loneliness were again his unwelcome companions.

After walking a short distance he remembered enough of the Twa's teachings to stem his immediate thirst and hunger. He sucked the moister from the leaves on trees, discovered grubs in the hollow of a rotten tree and a few burnt fruit hanging precariously to a scorched avocado tree. He intended to try and find his grandmother's village for there was a possibility she, or at least some of the Hutu villagers, would have survived

A small root of potatoes had escaped the notice of scavengers and, like a dog digging for a bone, Pascal finally unearthed a few grub infested tubers. These he rubbed against his tattered trousers to remove the soil before gnawing at them until his huger abated. The remainder he packed into a dry banana frond for he was not sure when he would find anything else to eat.

After two days he felt sure he was near his relatives' village; he'd spied several people during the day but kept silent and hidden. Being weak and frightened and well aware of imminent danger he continued stealthily through the forest like a hunted, wounded animal with feet transfixed at each snapping branch and bird's flight.

Eventually he recognised his surroundings and on reconnoitring saw a few huts which were intact apart from three burnt thatches. Two people, both of whom were relatives, stood in the shelter of a few trees. He tried to call his cousin's name but the words stuck in his throat, he was still afraid he would be heard by enemies. Slowly he moved forward.

Immediately he was recognised and clasped into warm, welcoming arms. No words were spoken for several minutes as tears rolled down the cheeks of both Pascal and his cousin. He was home at last and, hopefully, with people he could trust and who would shelter him if necessary. His family were, of course, all Hutus.

I saw Pascal for the last time early one morning. He was wearing a bright pink shirt the right sleeve rolled up just below what had once been an elbow. He had taken a walk to clear his headache and meet me as I made my way to work. He called and waved as I came into view and I noticed how fatigued he looked when we greeted one another. I felt his feverish forehead and suggested he returned home and took a couple of paracetamol which I produced from my emergency first aid kit. We sat chatting for a while then hugged before he decided to take my advice and return to his village. I turned and waved several times with a deep sense of foreboding.

News filtered through 'the jungle drums ' that Pascal was ill. I made my way to his village where I found him lying on reed matting, bathed in sweat, with a temperature of 104. Several solemn faced people stood in the doorway of his hut and I asked them for a bowl of cold water. Removing my head scarf I drenched it in the dubious looking liquid and, after wiping his face and chest, placed it across his glistening black forehead. His eyes flickered open but he didn't speak, he just squeezed my hand and smiled.

I had only a small bottle of water so a fire was lit to boil further water collected from a stream that day which, when cooled, would be one of the most important commodities to combat dehydration.

Throughout the late afternoon Pascal K managed to swallow paracetamol tablets and drink sips of boiled water; his temperature receded to 102. I took his hand and promised to obtain transport early the following morning in order he might receive hospital treatment then, before leaving to make the necessary arrangements, I asked his relative to administer water every two hours.

Pascal died in the early hours of the next morning.

Now there are only memories.

Chapter Seventeen

'Our memories are card indexes consulted,
and then put back in disorder
by authorities whom we do not control'

Cyril Connolly

Memories

Each time I visit Africa I experience intense emotions many of which bury themselves deeply and permanently within me then manifest themselves in a flash when a word or act triggers a memory......

Living with women who have been gang raped and with children who suffer the consequences of such atrocities.

- o o O o o - -

Enclosing an emaciated, silent child in one's arms while sad and weary parents, nearing the end of their endurance, sway to and fro as they heave enough volcanic rocks to make a hole in which to lay their dead baby. At twelve noon there was a family of seven, at twelve minutes past twelve there was only six.

- o o O o o - -

Night falling, after a crystal clear day, and spirals of smoke drifting through the village as cooking fires are lit and tended. Children gathering around the warm volcanic stones their scaly, spindly little legs snuggling close to gain the warmth these ancient, hard bedfellows emit. Distended stomachs noticeable as arms and fingers stretch and sighs of contentment relax the bones and bodies of children old before their time.

- o o O o o - -

Finding, in the dawn's early mist, elf like waifs huddled together in foetal positions around the volcanic rocks still warm from surrounding the previous night's cooking fire. All heads closely shaven and bodies attired in torn, ill fitting, inadequate clothing with colours as indeterminable as their sex, unless one lifts the rags a few inches above their jutting hip bones.

- o o 0 o o - -

Placing congealing lumps of the previous night's cold rice into small, dirty, cupped, eager hands, bringing life back to the mucous filled eyes of these ownerless spirits of the night.

- o o 0 o o - -

To hear, in the night, the screams of human beings who suffer the repercussions of rape and torture.

- o o 0 o o - -

Watching a disconsolate mother with three children suffering from malaria squatting around their cooking fire built from spindly twigs on which a blackened, battered aluminium pot warms a grey sludge – an excuse for a maize porridge evening meal.

- o o 0 o o - -

Several village children and I had been gathering wild avocados and the dried leaves underfoot crackled as Nathaniel approached us. His thin stooping body and tired eyes gave the impression life could stop at any moment and it would be of no consequence to him. I knew he still had the one child which had been badly wounded during the genocide. He had not remarried.

Nathaniel, a Hutu, and I had sat round the open fire that evening, after sharing our meal together, when he opened his heart to me and both he and I shed tears of sadness, anger and frustration as reality appeared like a devouring monster.

Nathaniel's Story

Nathaniel's naked, lithe body lay on the intricately woven rush mat which Pelagie, a Tutsi, had made for their wedding night five years before. His sleep was not sound and his limbs twitched in unison with the occasional troubled, jumbled answers his subconscious gave to Pelagie's questions.

Pelagie settled the two children one of whom was the orphaned son of Nathaniel's brother in Gisenyi. She shielded the flickering candle with her cupped palm as she made her way to Nathaniel then pinched its living flame between her finger and thumb casting the hut into darkness.

Before lying down she entwined her fingers tightly in prayer but, as on several occasions lately, words hadn't come easily for she wondered why her God had forsaken their nation. They were troubled times and many Tutsis had already been massacred.

Nathaniel and Pelagie's mud hut was a well kept, single, lonely, thatched dwelling in the foothills of the Virunga mountains and she prayed the Interahamwe wouldn't find their home that night. She kissed the nape of Nathaniel's neck and he turned and drew her body to his but neither was relaxed when their bodies entwined and it was midnight before they both fell into a restless sleep.

Nathaniel was away before dawn in his search for work and food for his family. He didn't disturb the children but kissed each one gently on the forehead before stroking his wife's smooth, brown cheek and quietly closing the hut door.

He returned late afternoon and was met by a neighbour who advised him not to return home or at least take a different route to normal. He would say no more as he hurried off into the trees.

Nathaniel's heart pounded as he ran towards his home not heeding the neighbour's advice.

There was no sound as he entered the clearing and several cooking pots and articles of clothing were scattered outside the hut. For several minutes he froze and his legs became lead weights not wanting to transfer him any nearer to the door which stood partly open. He knew he must go inside but his brain refused to accept what he might find.

Finally, moving haltingly forward, Nathaniel placed a trembling hand on the rickety door and pushed until it gaped wide open and there were the children, lying where he had left them, but in pools of blood. He turned to run tripping over the upended chair and went sprawling on the earth floor. Shouting his wife's name he crawled forward then, suddenly, slapped his hand over his mouth and gulped back the heart rending cries knowing the Interahamwe had found his home and might still be in the vicinity. With eyes closed and hands over both ears he tried to eradicate every sight and sound from his head as he stood up and blood pulsed through his body threatening to rupture every vein and artery.

His wife was gone.

Thoughts for the children finally returned and re-entering the hut he found his nephew was dead. His son was alive but had severe machete wounds to his left arm and leg.

He never found his wife.

- o o O o o - -

To counteract these profound memories there is always the immortal, awe-inspiring appearance each morning of the Virunga mountains, resplendent in their visionary gossamer shrouds behind which they attempt to shelter the ever diminishing families of mountain gorillas. These gentle, near human creatures are safe only if the jungle forest rangers find and destroy all the demonic traps laid during the night and apprehend the ever determined men whose furtive search for gorillas' hands, skulls and meat never ceases.

There can be misery and deprivation in the most beautiful settings.

I don't begrudge the tourists the stories they recount on their return from Africa of warm sunshine, exotic lodges, wonderful food and exciting safaris, but I do wonder how many will remember the poverty, suffering and hunger of the people they've encountered. Black children see, hear and feel pain and hunger exactly the same as white children although the western world doesn't always see, or want to see it that way. How can one eradicate such memories?

Nevertheless my heart rises each morning with the sun when the horizon grows lucid and small slivers of transparent clouds are pushed over the summits of Muhabura, Sabinyo and Karisimbe, and I pray it will be a day when we can make sure and steady progress for Rwanda, its people and creatures, and future experiences never duplicate those of the past.

Chapter Eighteen

'Africa demands tenacity but patience to the extreme'

Beatrice

A new rest house had been established in the foothills of the Virunga mountains and while working on a water pipeline in that area I decided to introduce myself to the manager, Beatrice.

The hotel provided accommodation for visitors wishing to climb a designated mountain, within the Parc National des Volcans, and meet groups of habituated mountain gorilla families. I was invited to stay the night and gratefully accepted for the last stretch of trenches dug that afternoon had been through a particularly rocky area and the day had proved long, hard and very hot.

The main single storey building, housing dining and rest room, was built with local stone; a terra cotta, tiled roof supported two tall chimneys. The chalet bedrooms were also of stone, had thatched roofs and were surrounded by various trees and a multitude of vibrant and varied flowers giving the whole compound a pleasant restful appearance. These small round chalets housed either double or twin beds and there was also a large dormitory sleeping twelve. Comfortable beds and clean linen greeted visitors as did spasmodic electricity - when there was sufficient diesel for the generator.

Two thatched open sided nyakats on the left of the drive-in provided shade when viewing the spectacular tree lined countryside to the southwest and the majestic mountains in the distance. A third small nyakat displayed hand woven basketry, carvings and artistic black and white cow dung paintings, all enticing visitors to purchase. Immediately in front of the rest house, towering over and enclosing the neighbouring village to the north are Sabinyo and Gahinga mountains; stretching out to the west into the troubled Democratic Republic of the Congo, are Karisoki and Bisoke, Muhabura disappearing to the east.

Although serviced by two, thirty two cubic metre tanks drawing their water from a source on Sabinyo, the water level had been extremely low for several weeks and on this particular evening we had been rationed to two mugs of water for drinking and none for personal ablutions. Beatrice had contacted the owners of the rest house - who presumably had influence in certain quarters - and had been promised a tanker containing water.

We each sacrificed a mug of water in order that we may enjoy a cup of tea and, after a meal of soup, maize bread and fruit we settled round a glowing log fire in the central fire place. Several officers joined us from the nearby barracks situated in the foothills, bringing their own water bottles. These barracks formed a line of defence between Rwanda and the DRC, the Virunga mountains being the border.

At 7pm rumblings, and an occasional muffled bang, could be heard; a vehicle of debatable vintage was approaching. We rushed out to see a tanker containing the much needed water. The two Japanese, who hoped to climb and find mountain gorillas the following morning, joined us in excited anticipation - cameras at the ready.

Our hearts sank! Most vehicles transporting visiting Japanese, Australian, American, English and various other tourists, were stout, four-wheeled drive affairs genuinely necessary if one wished to safely navigate the volcanic terrain and badly pitted tracks. The tanker was a rusty, ancient crock with one flat tyre and steam hissing from under its ill fitting bonnet.

The short, stocky driver battered his door with the flat of both hands then gave it a viscous kick before it gave way and he was able to jump down, followed closely by his colleague who had shuffled onto the driver's seat in order to vacate the vehicle; his door would not open. The outside handle was tied with a rope which disappeared through the open window into the vehicle and this was secured to the steering wheel shaft - perhaps the only stable part of the cab!

Luckily the generator was working but the track, on which the tanker had arrived, was some distance from the main building so we had little lighting with which to work. The two beautifully built, stone water tanks were situated a few feet from a hedge which ran along side this track. Both tanks had an inspection hatch in their concrete roof and it was into this orifice water was to be directed

On standing back I had an awful feeling this project was not going to be an easy one; the pipe from the tanker was situated much lower than the hatches. We were not going to get a constant flow of water unless the pump was in better condition than that of the tanker or some strong, healthy individual had exceptionally good lungs and a mouth with a diameter of six inches which could suck hard enough to get the water flowing - as one does when siphoning petrol!

One thing in our favour was the arrival of a small generator and two ark lights supplied by the soldiers.

Connecting the pipe to the tanker proved to be our first obstacle for both connections had rusted. We also needed ladders to gain access to the hatches in the water tanks.

By this time several local villagers and their families had arrived and were thoroughly enjoying the distraction from their normal early retirement to bed. A rather rickety ladder made from small trees was duly produced, a triangular affair with four rungs, the first rung about two foot six at the base the others tapering to a point. Two boys ascended this seven foot, unsteady but necessary piece of equipment and placed themselves, legs akimbo, ready to receive and insert the tanker pipe into the hatch. Unfortunately the pipe was not long enough and the tanker was unable get any closer to the water tanks due to a two foot drop between them! Work ceased; heads were scratched. Oh for a witch doctor or magic wand!

At 7.30pm it was finally decided the water needed to be transferred manually so every available container, large and small, was commissioned. Staff, villagers and soldiers disappeared in all directions and reappeared with a motley, but most welcome, selection of containers. Two children brought their plastic drinking mugs!

A chain gang was organised which commenced near the tanker and continued up the ladder. The largest receptacles were placed on the ground, filled with water from the tanker, then buckets, saucepans and bowls were dipped in and handed up the ladder until the water finally found its way down the hatches.

Unfortunately the pressure mechanism and shut off valve on the tanker could not be controlled extremely well consequently the large containers continually overflowed. There was soon a quagmire and we were wallowing in a mud bath of which any health spa would have been proud. Those of us, handing water up the ladder, were soon drenched to the skin and, unfortunately, only half the tanker's cargo reached its destination.

With the tanker depleted and entertainment over for the night our audience gradually retired to their homes with stories to be related throughout the whole area, no doubt much elaborated, for weeks to come.

On returning to the guest house I had to make do with a saucepan of water with which to wash so I stripped down to pants and bra and Beatrice poured the 'gold dust' over my head while I stood in a washing up bowl. The water captured in the bowl had to suffice to rid my feet and legs of mud! Visitors were, of course, given priority but requested to be as frugal as possible with their ablutions.

Another tanker had been promised for the following night but, as I had to return to trench digging the next morning and home to my village in the late afternoon, I was not involved with any further water sports.

I did return to the rest house a few days before returning to the UK and, as Beatrice's accommodation was a twin bedded chalet I was invited to spend the last night with her. We talked well into the night and I was shocked to hear further stories of the genocide during which her husband had been killed. Tears appeared, her throat constricted - this was the case with so many who wanted to talk to me of their troubled lives. Luckily her three children were in Kenya with grandparents when the genocide began and did not return to Rwanda until mid-nineteen ninety five.

It must have been 3am before we finally went to sleep.

I was awakened before dawn with the trilling of Beatrice's mobile phone. She swung her legs over the side of the bed and I could see the look of consternation on her face as she listened to the incoming call. This was in Kinyarwanda so I understood very little of the conversation apart from the fact that there was a problem or trouble somewhere. A few minutes later the line went dead and Beatrice was unable to reconnect.

The call had been from a Pastor who was endeavouring to help families being hunted and killed on the other side of the mountain range in the DRC their only vice being the fact they were Tutsis born in the DRC and spoke Kinyarwanda. Many people within these mountain borders spoke Kinyarwanda and suffered the same fate.

There was nothing we could do. Beatrice advised the families to try and find hiding places, if possible until dark, then endeavour to make their way east to the Ugandan border. Once in Uganda they would be safe and could then head south into Rwanda where sanctuary would be found.

We heard no more from the Pastor or his people.

Beatrice was an angel in disguise for she helped many desperate people from the DRC. She adopted orphans from the genocide, collected clothes for vulnerable families in her district and fed their children, also set up women's craft groups the products of which were sold to tourists visiting the guest house and mountain gorillas.

We became firm friends Beatrice and I, and this little guest house became a haven for me whenever I had time to visit.

Post Script - Unfortunately, Beatrice suffered with a heart problem and sadly passed away before this book was published. A dear friend who will always be remembered.

1: Sick baby restored to good health - note disfigured forefinger (Chapter 10)

2: Cutting planks in Virunga foothills (Chapter 11)

3: Digging trench for water pipeline (Chapter 11)

4: Pipeline being laid (Chapter 11)

5: Emmanuel's simple home (Chapter 12)

6: Family Planning Meeting (Chapter 13)

7: Silver Back Mountain Gorilla (Chapter 19)

8: Batwa Dwelling (Chapter 21)

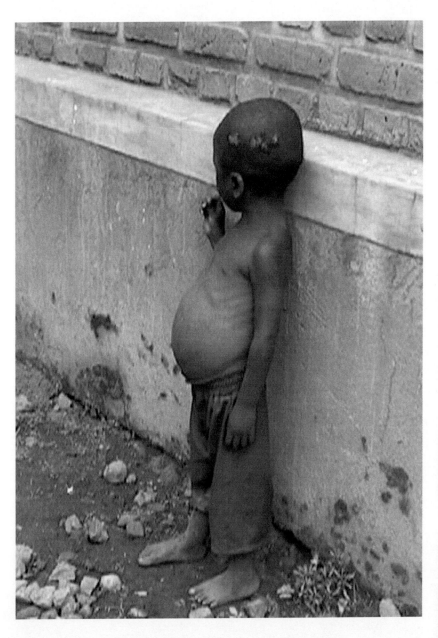

9: 'My Little Old Man' (Chapter 22)

10: Stones for Water Tank Foundations (Chapter 24)

11: Cyungugu Earthquake Destroys School (Chapter 24)

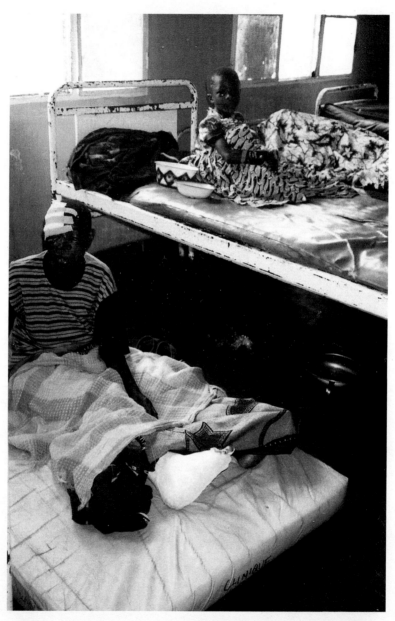

**12: Victims of Cyungugu earthquake recover in hospital
(Chapter 24)**

13: Jeannie's burnt hand (Chapter 25)

14: New clothes and sugar cane for New Year (Chapter 35)

Chapter Nineteen

Muhabura, Sabinyo, Karisimbi, Bisoke, they are all fighting for their lives and that of the few remaining trees and creatures existing in these beautiful celestial peaks. They have witnessed it all; beheading; gentle caresses; extreme courage; inhumanity to man, woman, child and beast. Their gigantic green eyes only had to blink and the scene changed; another horrific act took place. They accede to the adverse elements for the rain revives their parched roots; the wind plucks their leaves to the ground to nurture the saplings who, in their teenage years will save the life-giving slopes from erosion, but they are unable to accept man's heartless, vicious and brutal aggression towards them and the creatures they nourish and shelter.

DJR

Mountain Gorillas

Rwanda is often called Little Switzerland with its numerous majestic mountains and fertile valleys which were once blanketed with a multitude of tall, dignified ancient trees, mountain gorillas, elephants, antelope, buffalo and many other species. Much of the lower dark forests have been stripped to make room for agriculture, and the two hundred year old giants and bamboo turned into tables and chairs for the 'civilised world's' dining rooms and conservatories.

The steep mountain slopes have experienced their own inexorable genocide. They have been slashed and cut, their life blood drained almost to their summits; the ensuing terraces now resemble a monster's stairway up which Rwandans struggle daily to till the earth in an endeavour to sustain their large families.

While working on a pipeline in the foothills of Muhabura I was given the privileged opportunity of climbing and studying the mountain gorillas whom the government, and indigenous population, now realise are an excellent source of income - tourism, hopefully, saving these gentle creatures from extinction.

Before the climb I decided to stay at Beatrice's small guest house and on entering was greeted by the usual glowing, central log fire crackling and spitting in readiness to counteract the chill which accompanies a damp evening in the foothills of the Virungas. Two American's and I were to be ready by 5.30 the next morning for our climb.

Having visited the mountain gorillas that day a party of Dutchmen recounted their vivid experiences while we all sat with hands clamped around mugs of hot chocolate and eating bread toasted on the roaring fire; Sugar, the cook, and Rosie making sure our mugs were regularly replenished. Rosie, a well built waitress-come-general-help, was never without a broad smile and when we met always wanted to know if I had found her a Mzungu fiancée - with plenty of dollars!

Although in most convivial and interesting company I said my 'Goodnights' early and left while the evening was in full swing. I knew the climb next day would not be easy and I needed a good night's rest.

Waking before my alarm I looked out to see the moon, a silver coin disappearing teasingly out of dawn's grasp. A cursory, but very refreshing, cold shower left me shivering so I entered the dining area with hands tucked into the armpits of a warm, woolly jumper knowing I would need to discard such creature comforts at sun up.

After breakfasting on omelette, toasted maize bread and steaming hot coffee we joined the rangers and the American's pristine 4 x 4 standing ready to take us into the foothills.

My day pack was light, it consisted of a litre of boiled water, an extra pair of dry socks, a maize cob, muesli bar, a banana, dextro tablets, emergency first aid kit and camera.

En route we visited the Park's office for our entry permits and briefing from the head ranger.

'When entering the Park your voices are to be kept low, no flash cameras and five metres distance to be kept from the gorillas.' (This is not always possible as we were to find out). 'Anyone with a cough, cold, diarrhoea or any other complaint liable to infect the gorillas is not allowed to climb; clearly no one is under 15 years of age.' He waited for a few seconds before continuing obviously awaiting any comments.

The two Americans turned to each other and nodded. I sincerely hoped they were both nodding the truth for human diseases can kill mountain gorillas en bloc. A Swiss couple was also part of our group and the girl, I noticed, kept her distance for she was smoking.

Our Americans were 'doing Africa' and suggested the oldest of our group climbing Sabinyo, which of course was me, should set the pace so that no one would be left behind. Not that the rangers would allow anyone to be left anywhere. The lead ranger gave me a wink and so the party set off.

My first encounters with mountain gorillas proved the most exciting experiences of my life. That was many years ago on Mgahinga and in Bwindi's Impenetrable Forest in Uganda. In recent years I had visited these wonderful gentle creatures on several occasions in the Parc Nationale des Volcans in Northern Rwanda and each time the adrenalin flowed and my heart beat faster when I knew we were close to a family. This time was to be no exception.

The day dawned fresh and cool, free from pollution and noise. There was still a slight drizzle and we knew the going would not be easy for it was muddy and the residue of rain from the trees and shrubbery soaked our clothing. Fortunately, the storm clouds scudded away to the east and the sky cleared; the day promised well.

Sabinyo's summit, segregated from its lower slopes by a pathway of transient clouds, embellished binary silhouettes gliding freely near its peak having found early morning thermals. I could almost smell the munching, mating, sucking, playful gorilla families in their mountain retreat safe for the day from guns, traps and machetes.

A long, gradual, exposed climb was necessary before the gradient of Sabinyo began and our boots were soon clogged with mud. This we scraped off with a short, stout stick not wanting them to turn into ton weights.

I noticed both Americans were sweating profusely before we even began the actual mountain climb so set, what I thought, was a reasonably leisurely pace once we were out of the foothills.

Long before the first scheduled stop our Americans were lagging well behind, bent at the waist, hands on hips, panting and calling as quietly as possible, 'We need…..ah..… to stop…for water.'

Our ranger took this opportunity, as with our many other 'rests,' to inform us of the habits of mountain gorillas and the various other animals we may be fortunate enough to encounter and, although eager to find these creatures, I was always intrigued with the passionate way in which the rangers imparted their knowledge.

'The mountain gorilla's habitat,' he said, going from standing to squat position, 'Ranges from the base of the foothills to over 4,000 metres. This variation causes a wide range of vegetation and forest types. Unfortunately, a vast sea of cleaned agricultural land now surrounds this small island of gorilla forest habitat, consequently, only about 300 mountain gorillas remain in Rwanda.'

Our Swiss smoker squatted on her haunches and in perfect English asked, 'Ok if I take a cigarette? She was politely, but firmly, informed she must wait until she returned to the guest house. Although his reply was grudgingly received Alphonse, unruffled, continued, 'One usually encounters only Eastern or Western Lowland gorillas in zoos because mountain gorillas do not survive in captivity.'

Having tucked trousers into my ten year old, but most comfortable, boots and rolled down shirt sleeves we pressed on for a further two hours through thick forest, thorny branches and bracken endeavouring to avoid any critters who may provide a bite not unlike a cigarette burn. Barring our way were vicious eight foot stinging nettles which could leave one scratching for days if touched. I felt sure the Americans could look forward to a sleepless night for they wore Bermuda length shorts, T-shirts and sneakers topped with three quarter white socks. The Swiss couple was exquisitely attired but their expensive beige suede boots no longer looked expensive.

Our ranger pointed out several gorilla nests and quietly whispered, 'The family were here a short time ago,' and picking up a dark, chocolate coloured stool handed it to our Swiss visitor who had just moved up from the rear of the group. 'Look it's still warm,' he told her. She instinctively extended her hand but then, with an 'Oh, Non!' immediately withdrew it suddenly realizing what she was accepting.

Alphonse retrieved the shattered specimen, trying desperately not to smile and, placing it on a bed of leaves, passed it round for inspection pointing out the various undigested seeds which would probably take root.

Unfortunately, these elusive creatures decided to cross a ravine which proved impossible for humans to traverse unless one had either the dexterity of a mountain goat or the climbing ability of a gorilla. By this time the Americans were exhausted and insisted they could go no farther. The younger of the two, gasping for breath and wet with sweat, tiredly informed us, 'I'll wait here until the gorillas return.' Our ranger politely informed him, 'Unfortunately they probably won't return this same way and, if they do, it will not be for days. I have a contingent of armed soldiers with walkie-talkies escorting our party at a distance but all will need to proceed with us; no one can be left unaccompanied.' The Swiss girl had been coughing during the climb and our guide moved back along the line and had a quiet word with her before we continued climbing.

Another ten minute rest period was called only to find the boys had drunk all their water. The rangers don't carry water; one is instructed at the briefing to carry enough water for the climb.

I relinquished a few swallows from my bottle and we again moved on finally reaching the ravine summit, this enabled the group to ease its way through dense undergrowth to a descending track leading, hopefully, to the gorillas.

During this descent we encountered inquisitive golden monkeys their coats glistening as the sun's rays swept their agile bodies. They bounced through the branches of immature trees whose roots were making desperate attempts to obtain a footing on the rocky outcrop of the ravine.

We were all feeling tired so a further five minute halt revived our aching knees during which Alphonse introduced us to the gorilla's staple diet and eating habits. 'Mountain gorillas' he said, 'Are primarily vegetarians and the bulk of their diet is galium. Many other plants, roots and flowers are enjoyed including the bark from hagenia trees but their speciality is new bamboo shoots available only during the two rainy seasons.'

A bored look entered the eyes of our smoker and I think the need for nicotine was beginning to kick in. Nevertheless, our ranger continued with his information.

'The gorillas obtain all the necessary liquid from plants, trees and decaying wood, which is also a source of nutrients, they don't drink.' He then demonstrated the quantity of water that could be extracted from such as tiso leaves by picking a selection and squeezing them between both hands - there was enough for two of us to drink a sample.

'As you can see the juicy, wild celery is giant sized but is effortlessly uprooted by these creatures then stripped of its leaves and peeled; it's impossible for the hollow stems to be eaten quietly. Methodical crunching is interspersed with curious whining singing, expressive grunts of contentment and further bursts of song, which you will probably hear, and explosive long farts which you will most certainly smell when we meet the family.'

We came across old nests near which gorillas had defecated then snuggled down for the night; as a safety precaution nests are only ever used once. Researchers, we were informed, often estimated group sizes and ages by the size and number of faeces.

Two members of a descending Flora and Fauna Spanish film crew, together with a ranger, met us. The well built, handsome but heavily sweating Spaniard had his left arm in a makeshift sling with blood staining the area where a bandaged forefinger poked out. This, we heard, had been sliced through with a machete while hacking out a path ready for filming. He now needed urgent medical attention which, unfortunately, was many hours away. His accompanying ranger had picked up the finger and immediately introduced it to the hand and, using the film crew's first aid kit, had bandaged it and was now anxious to get the poor man to Ruhengeri hospital the centre renowned for sewing back limbs during the genocide!

After about four hours the lead ranger called us to an abrupt halt by raising his right hand. He whispered into his two-way radio making contact with the armed soldiers scouting some distance from the main party. These, I knew, were more for our safety against insurgents than wild animals; it was 2002 and all visitors to the Virungas were heavily guarded.

Some climbs can prove extremely frustrating if it's raining and the family is hidden - ensconced in thick forest and undergrowth for shelter. One hears only the snapping of twigs or the sight of a solitary black furry arm extended through grey/green dripping ferns as it reaches for a luscious shoot or branch. On this occasion the setting was idyllic.

Our guide turned again placing a forefinger over his closed lips; camouflaged amongst the branches was a mass of moving black. The family was a few metres away so we left everything (including the Swiss girl) apart from our cameras, with the soldiers and crept cautiously forward.

'Oh look,' shouted one American.

A long withering glare was thrown in the American's direction as a large black hand appeared as if by magic. We stood rooted to the spot until the group settled; Alphonse walked slowly forward talking quietly to a family of fifteen Sabinyo mountain gorillas.

Rwandan rangers have spent many years habituating these creatures, interacting daily with them and returning their guttural grunts and sounds thus building a unique relationship between man and wild beast.

All aches, pains and moans were forgotten as we entered a clearing. I was well pleased to notice Waldrow, one of our Americans, covered his mouth with his hand as he turned his head and stifled a slight cough.

The scene was of outstanding beauty and tranquillity. The warm sunlight meandered through the moving branches of mature trees, throwing a kaleidoscope of dancing medallions onto the forest floor and mingling with these wild but gentle giants. The family included a superb silverback lying on one side, his majestic head supported by a massive leathery black hand; two nursing females with their babies sat close by.

Papa silverback nonchalantly blinked his deep, amber eyes, altered his position slightly to get a better view of the intruders and uttered several grunts, Alphonse answering, I'm sure in the affirmative, indicating all was well. A carefree air pervaded over the whole family and I watched mesmerised for the next hour. Oh! to have exchanged a few weeks with Dian Fossey during her lifetime.

I suddenly realized Alphonse had moved silently behind me and placing his hands on my shoulders whispered, 'Would you like to say hello to Munane?'

I nodded and murmured, 'Muraho Munane.'

Alphonse whispered again, 'Do as I do and then squat averting eye contact.'

He moved very slowly forward constantly talking gorilla talk. I followed endeavouring to mimic his moves and sounds.

We stopped within about two meters of the small group and slowly squatted. Alphonse half turned his head towards Papa, as did I, and unblinking eyes, thought provoking and curious met mine for a few seconds. Occasionally Munane's head wandered slightly to one side then nonchalantly upwards as though thinking and experiencing a feeling of déjà vu. Those soft dark eyes were totally devoid of anger, fear or distrust and I felt more an object of calm and curious contemplation than a threat to his family.

This magnificent silverback was huge and weighed in at approximately 200 kilograms. The body was covered with dense black hair and a silver saddle straddled the back waistline, the feet and hands mimicking human hands but much larger. The females were half their husband's size and the babies, I was told, weighed in at about two kilograms at birth. For several months the hair on their head sticks straight up looking as though they have been given an electric shock and their big eyes register constant surprise.

The two mothers moved to sit beside a stream rippling down a slight incline where juveniles gathered fallen leaves and chucked them into the water. Other youngsters were trying to catch the tiny flotilla before it disappeared from sight, issuing squeals of delight as they threw any captured 'boats' at one another and at the placid mothers who, finally, decided to move back with Munane.

A wide-eyed baby cradled in its mother's arms held tenaciously to a vastly extended teat while endeavouring to watch the water sports. The mother eventually decided her teat had been stretched to its limit so placing her hand gently at the back of the baby's head she tried to bring it back against her breast. The infant was having none of it with the consequence the teat shot from the baby's mouth mimicking a released elastic band. The infant tried once more to turn, having latched again onto its source of food, but was prevented from doing so in no uncertain terms!

Nyakarima, a juvenile, suddenly dropped from a nearby tree and beat the ground with his branch as he scampered across the clearing, bark and leaves flying everywhere. Reaching a ranger he whacked him across the shins before returning to his companion in the trees. They both shook the branches vigorously and whooped with delight; I was sure the smiling ranger would display a good sized bruise by morning.

Munane rolled onto his back, hands behind his head when Gasindikira, a two year old, sidled up beside him ready for play, but Papa grunted and pushed her unceremoniously away, no one was going to disturb his forty winks. Our ranger signalled it was time for us to leave.

I peered over my shoulder for as long as possible to catch the last glimpses of this intoxicating Sabinyo family and hoped it wouldn't be too long before we'd meet again.

We collected our gear - and the Swiss girl - from the soldiers, she certainly wasn't very happy. Her boyfriend attempted to placate her on his return by showing her pictures on his camera which I feel only made matters worse. Alphonse had, presumably, refused her entrance to the clearing because of her cough.

Under foot was slippery and much of our descent was spent on our posteriors with rangers grabbing shirt collars and trouser waist bands. The Americans couldn't wait to impart the day's experience to a group of new arrivals from Japan as we quaffed the steaming hot, sweet tea with which Beatrice greeted us on our return. We heard the wounded Spaniard was out of hospital and the doctors had stitched back the severed finger!

My best record of the day proved to be a 'likeness' of a four month old, wide eyed baby gorilla looking straight into my lens, hair expertly spiked! The best offer of the day was from the Americans who provided me with a lift to my base at Imbaraga where I was to pack in readiness for my return to the UK the next day.

Chapter Twenty

'There is nothing like returning
to a place that remains unchanged to find the ways in
which you yourself have altered'

Nelson Mandela

A Return to the UK

As I had to spend a night in Nairobi before returning to England Fee, an old friend en-route for South Africa, asked if I would meet at her hotel so that we could have a meal together. Although we had kept in touch I had not seen Fee since working with her in the rain forests of Borneo four years earlier.

I was limited for time and knew travelling through Nairobi to the Gregoire Kaybanda International Airport during the evening rush hour was not going to be the easiest of journeys; I had about ninety minutes with Fee before my taxi arrived.

The restaurant was full but a waiter soon took our order. Unfortunately it was nearly an hour before an excellent fish dish was placed before us which cut my eating time down considerably. I left Fee still chewing, for she was not leaving Nairobi until the next morning, and hurried to the foyer to find the waiting taxi.

It was an interesting, exciting journey nipping into non existent gaps; driving on the centre reservation doing 50 mph; passing slow moving and sometimes stationery traffic; horns blared and fists were shaken through numerous vehicles' open windows. I closed my eyes and tried not to think what would happen should we pass a police car.

I arrived safely - and early - for my flight so booked in, off-loaded the old canvas hold all and retained only my hand luggage, placing my passport and boarding card safely in the side pocket of my trousers.

On my way to the duty free I felt a peculiar churning in my stomach and decided I must make for the 'ladies' - immediately! I stopped an official looking man in navy blue uniform sporting an airport badge on which his name was printed.

'David,' I said, trying to look unconcerned, 'Where are the ladies' toilets please?' An extended arm, ending with an index finger pointing towards the end of a very long concourse, was held in position for a few seconds, 'Down there madam,' said David before lowering the pointed finger and saluting.

I was unable to move immediately and knew I was in dire trouble. Keeping my buttocks and inside thighs squeezed tightly together I finally moved with slow, deliberate, minute steps, my whole body swaying slightly to the right and left as I walked, duplicating the catwalk stroll. The concourse seemed never ending and beads of sweat formed on my forehead as I realized I was not going to make it. Suddenly the illuminated, childish pictures depicting the toilets were just a few yards in front of me. It was then that my inside exploded - everything seemed to give way - I had no control whatsoever! I lunged into a cubicle and felt the warmth of the undigested fish meal spread down the back of my legs as I was violently sick! All I could do was to strip off and sit on the toilet.

When the vomiting and diarrhoea finally ceased I used reams of toilet paper and water, from continual flushing of the toilet, to clean myself, my sneakers and the floor - my knickers and socks I flushed down the toilet.

Standing naked apart from a T-shirt and bra, I thought what the hell do I do now? My luggage had been checked in. I had never heard of a streaker being permitted to board an airline! I put my head round the toilet door and called out several times, 'Anyone about?'

Luckily an on-duty attendant finally arrived, who spoke a little English, to whom I explained the situation. She said she would need the boarding ticket to retrieve my luggage if I was to find something to wear. It was then I remembered the boarding ticket, together with my passport, was in a trouser pocket! Delicately I unfolded the stinking trousers and fished in the appropriate pocket to produce a smelly, damp passport and boarding pass.

The attendant brought me a bowl of warm water with which to finalise my ablutions and swill the documents before she dried them under the hand dryer. Luckily the passport's hard outside cover had protected it so the inside pages had not suffered too badly. The attendant hurried away, clutching the barely legible boarding pass and slightly soggy passport, to retrieve my stalwart old hold all.

I sat on the lid of the toilet and within half an hour she was back with my luggage and I was able to clothe myself reasonably respectably. I say reasonably respectably because I had given most of my clothing away before leaving Rwanda so had only a pair of ancient green work trousers and no socks; luckily a couple of pairs of knickers were tucked in my wash bag. Nevertheless I was clean, mobile and ready to return my luggage to the check in.

Two black nurses were waiting for me as I left the 'ladies' and informed me I would be unable to fly due to my diarrhoea and sickness - airline regulations. I assured them I felt fine and must be on that plane. They took me to a surgery and said I should stay while they administered several varying sized coloured tablets and see how things progressed.

I improved sufficiently over the next hour for them to agree not to inform the airline if I promised to take the prescribed tablets every four hours during the flight and for four days on returning home. This I agreed to do and was charged $20.00 and given no receipt. On returning to the loading bay with my luggage I was again checked in and made my way through the x-ray machines to the waiting room.

We traversed the last checkpoint - boarding imminent - and the attendant looked at my boarding pass, scrutinized it closely and said, 'What happened to this?'

To which I replied, 'Don't ask.'

He smiled and ushered me forward.

On entering the plane one of the flight crew, directing passengers to their seats, gave me and my pass a quizzical look and then asked a pretty young Kenyan flight attendant to show me to my seat. I had been up-graded to first class! Why and how I had no idea.

Endeavouring to give the impression I always travelled first class attired thus I sauntered forward in faded green cotton trousers and trainers that were still extremely soggy. Luckily I was placed in the first window seat in the left aisle so did not have to pass the other passengers. These, I later noticed, were in beautiful tailored costumes and designer blouses or sophisticated dresses adorned with their best jewellery, nails manicured and hair coiffured, no doubt, in one of Nairobi's top salons. Several men wore Savile Row suits and pristine white, or blue and white striped open necked shirts, others had cashmere pullovers thrown nonchalantly over their shoulders; tailored Armani slacks completed various ensembles.

Adjacent, and facing me in the aisle seat, was what I assumed to be a businessman, a diplomat or someone as equally important. On settling into his seat he produced a multitude of papers and a gold pen, the top of which he continually clicked although he was not using it at that stage to write anything.

Until the plane took off I was occupied with trying all the refinements which make first class so very, very different from economy. On pressing a bed button the back of my extra wide seat slowly moved backwards, I had already found the button for supporting my legs and feet thus changing the whole contraption into a full length bed. Other buttons lit extra lighting both over and at the rear of the seat; called the stewards; produced a television and, most conveniently, brought up a fan-like screen between me and my very 'important person.'

Before we took off I was offered a variety of nibbles and my first English language newspaper for three months. The bar, I was informed, would be available soon after we were in flight. After three months in the wilds of Rwanda, the disastrous affects of the meal in the Nairobi hotel and now first class travel, I had gone from one extreme of living to another in a matter of twenty four hours!

The plane's engines purred into action and I settled down to watch the evening sky gradually turn from an azure blue, to apricot and red, violet and midnight. The stars sent their never ending journey of light from outer space as I snuggled my shoulders and elbows into the seat's plush upholstery while accepting a five star menu from a pleasant cabin crew. Remembering my earlier embarrassing experience at the airport I was modest in my request ordering a small salad with wholemeal roll. A cheese board with seven varieties of cheese appeared almost immediately with a selection of biscuits, butter pats or Flora, and a glass of port. I could have had any alcoholic drink I chose, including champagne, but opted for mineral water and later a very weak coffee. The bar and snacks were available throughout the flight, as well as four-course meals, but I puffed up the spotless white pillows, drew a soft, sweet smelling blanket under my chin, pressed the appropriate buttons and slept in delightful comfort until I was awakened for breakfast at 4.30am. This proved every bit as varied and enjoyable as the previous meals made even more so because I was feeling fine and able to eat everything ordered and put before me.

Feeling replenished and totally relaxed I inspected my complimentary toilet bag and decided to take it, and myself, to view a first class airline bathroom. I was not disappointed.

By the time I returned to my seat my face shone, my armpits exuded an exotic aroma - the name of which I cannot remember - my teeth were a sparkling white and my feet were enjoying the delights of new, soft, dry socks each one depicting a loiter of leopard footprints across the toes.

As we had a further hour before touch down at London Heathrow, and I was fully awake, I decided to make a list of items to be included on the agenda of our next executive meeting of the David Rundle Trust. I also studied an interesting report on the Rwandan mountain Batwa people and widows of Gasiza, they were definitely people to be visited and, possibly, included in our list of future projects.

Chapter Twenty One

'Although the world is full of suffering,
it is also full of the overcoming of suffering'
Helen Keller

Widows of Gasiza and the Batwa Mountain People

A few days after returning to Rwanda I managed to acquire a friend who, on several Sundays, procured the use of a dilapidated, open backed van in exchange for a small remuneration and a few litres of petrol. I had been asked to visit the women of Gasiza, (widowed through the genocide) also the Batwa mountain people, so took full advantage of the offer of motorised transport for both venues were some distance from my base at that time.

Francois collected me about 8.20am and we first visited the partially constructed petrol station situated at the top end of Ruhengeri town on the road to Kigali. This depot sported a large concrete forecourt and we found ourselves waiting for about five minutes in front of two petrol pumps, of questionable origin, before an attractive, well proportioned lady in tight jeans, navy blue diaphanous blouse and dangerously high heeled, well worn, gold strapped sandals approached our van. We asked her for 10,000 francs worth of petrol.

'Would you please wait for further customers because it's not worth starting the generator for just one vehicle,' she requested with a seductive smile which harmonised extremely well with her revealing attire.

Francois, a sturdy, dark skinned, forty five to fifty year old, nodded his agreement. Presumably, this was the normal procedure for he made no complaint to our buxom forecourt attendant (possible owner) or excuses to me. We sat patiently chatting while two further cars, a motor bike and a small lorry finally joined our cavalcade before our lady, in her hazardous gold sandals, hobbled towards us and enquired what quantity of fuel was required. The total volume could not have been sufficient for she shook her head and staggered precariously back to her headquarters and settled into a faded red armchair. Everyone, all male drivers, seemed completely content to wait - and watch.

Another car arrived; by this time it was nearly nine o'clock. Heaving herself from the comfort of her armchair the attendant disappeared through a door at the rear of the building and soon the spasmodic grunts of a generator could be heard. The necessary connection was finally made and life induced we hoped, at least until the waiting vehicles had been fed.

We were served first and entertained, at no extra cost, with a Rwandan rendition of a tune resembling a Beatles' recording, one golden sandaled foot tapping; portly shoulders and ample bosoms jigging up and down in time with the animated nozzle placed haphazardly into our petrol tank. Luckily the secreted generator continued to chug along happily adding a vibrant beat to the melodious rendering.

I produced the necessary francs, was given a hand written receipt, and we were soon on our way with a friendly wave from both our model-in-the-making and the drivers and their passengers in the remaining vehicles.

The journey to Gasiza was pleasant enough for the main road was reasonable the Chinese having recently carried out resurfacing, that is until we reached our turning for Gasiza. From then on I thought we would certainly be stranded with broken springs or at least a puncture for the gradually inclining, pot holed track soon became extremely steep and we were not equipped with anything as modern as four wheel drive or a spare wheel. More danger also lay in the number of children hanging onto the rear of the vehicle and running alongside as we passed through several villages. We were afraid to stop and admonish them for fear of getting bogged down in the clay. Many children in the outlying districts so seldom see a car they think it's great fun to chase or try to beg a ride by holding on to a tailboard whenever there is an opportunity.

En route we passed scattered villages whose dwellings had either corrugated or thatched roofs, finally stopping at a spring where dozens of children were collecting water from a corroded pipe jutting from a steep bank at the side of the track. Their motley collection of coloured containers was in stark contrast to the children's garments whose colours had long since parted company with the material; no one wore shoes. The slow trickle of water emanating from this spring took approximately fifteen minutes to fill a twenty-five litre canister and the hollow near the outlet had become a quagmire in which the children had to stand as they moved up the queue.

While taking photographs I noticed the difficulty some of the smaller ones experienced when trying to lift their precious cargo onto shaven heads. Some enlisted the help of older children when they found it impossible to get the containers into position. I had my doubts whether many would have much water left after walking several kilometres to their individual villages. As they began their homeward journey water trickled onto their ragged T-shirted shoulders and down their straining backs, this was due to holes in the containers and the ill fitting, burgundy coloured bungs made from the large tapered buds from banana trees.

News of our visit reached the ears of a village chief and he was soon on the scene wanting to know if I could install a piped water supply with a robinet (tap) in his village. He'd heard all about our water projects. I was intrigued as to the type of communication system they had installed for news of our work had reached areas miles from anywhere with no visible cables, wires, telephones or transport. Someone, perhaps, had a good set of jungle drums!

I tried to explain the project would prove expensive, due to the distance, transport - and rugged terrain, but my words fell on deaf ears. Before we could leave I had to promise at least a return visit before I left for the UK.

We resumed our bone bruising journey passing village women clothed in varied, boldly coloured gukenyeras, some chatting, some singing, many carrying the familiar sleeping bundles on their backs. In their bright attire and balancing yellow plastic containers on their turbaned heads they resembled a flotilla of butterflies as they wound their way gracefully to and from a water source. Their posture is enviable; everything, apart from babies, is carried on their heads, this includes gaily patterned umbrellas, hundred weights of charcoal or potatoes and their beautifully crafted baskets. Their heads are shielded with an ingata - a stout ring woven from banana or some such fronds

In the fields women were swinging heavy hoes while they prepared the soil, or bent double as they planted their crops. None would have any problem touching their toes without bent knees.

Few families are lucky enough to own a cow but some have goats and it is the children who usually cut fodder or escort these animals daily to find grazing. Once cut this crop is carried on their heads so drapes over the whole of their bodies and renders them almost invisible, all one can see are two shoeless feet marching methodically forward under a 'thatch.'

I now understand why most African babies are born with a vast mop of thick black hair; tiny heads are usually exposed to the searing sun for hours when strapped to their mothers' backs.

Periodically a working mother will lay down her hoe, undo the large knots of material tied across the top of her bosom and around her waist thus releasing the baby strapped to her back. Then, swinging the infant around and forward by one of its arms (exactly the same movement a female gorilla employs with her infant) the child is stretched several times, by pulling both arms and legs, then held aloft before it is returned to the mother's back and secured into position - exercise over! Unfortunately, this makes them lazy little critters who don't want to walk much until they are well over eighteen months old, they scream if put down. The child carried in this way rarely sees anything but the mother's back and is, therefore, starved of connecting with items, movement, colours and the usual daily interests our babies encounter.

We stopped in the market to buy baked potatoes cooked on an open fire and I noticed a little girl, of about three years old, with a white cloth tied around her which bulged at the back. I was astonished to think a mother would allow such a young child to carry a baby having previously noticed some young girls had a deformity in the lower back which I presumed was from piggy-backing younger siblings for many hours a day at an early age. Approaching the little girl with a proffered bonbon I peeked inside the cloth, it was a beautifully carved wooden effigy of a baby mountain gorilla!

The scenery was spectacular as we neared Lake Karago lying in a sun drenched valley surrounded with wooded slopes on three sides, the Virunga mountains providing a protective back drop in the distance. Parking near the lake we were soon surrounded by a curious multitude all wanting to shake hands and show the way to a sturdy brick building in which I was to give a talk on birth control, family planning and AIDS and present the widowed women of

Gasiza with a gift of five new fishing nets.

There was a tremendous roar and clapping as I distributed the gifts and the inevitable singing and dancing ensued for the next half hour. Babies strapped to jigging backs continued, as always, to sleep through it all.

With the nets ceremoniously distributed I placed the box of condoms at the ready these having passed the all seeing eyes of customs without any questions being asked. I often wondered what the customs' officers would have said if they had decided to search the elderly Mzungu's luggage. As well as dozens of condoms I also carried chisels, a hammer and a medium sized saw! I had my story ready should I be questioned; the condoms were to be distributed during the birth control sessions; the saw might come in useful should the men refuse to use condoms!

Near the lake was an army barracks with the consequence the women's meagre income, from fishing the lake and growing potatoes, was sometimes supplemented, hence the necessity for instruction on condoms and AIDS. How does one enlighten a room full of widows in the use of such an item when they have never heard of, seen or used one before – and in a foreign language! I had come prepared; I had had a well endowed, black, wooden penis carved.

Francois of course spoke Kinyarwanda but his English was ragged and my French equally so, but between us we managed to enlighten our crowd of a hundred or so enthralled ladies on the benefits of using condoms if they felt it absolutely necessary to entertain the soldiers. We began with serious instruction on birth control and family planning. Most knew that 'entertaining' could result in pregnancy but were ignorant of how their internal organs worked so we reverted to basics before tackling the subject of AIDS.

Finally it was time to let the genie out of the bottle. Giggles and yelps of laughter filled the room until we finally settled down to the fact that these transparent, elasticised items were extremely important if a killer was to be eradicated. There was no lack of volunteers to emulate our demonstration with the carving and it was obvious, by their studious, wide eyed manipulation of this object and the condoms, that our teaching had not been in vain. We stressed that the women should educate the soldiers to the fact, 'No condom; no entertainment.'

Before continuing our journey to the Batwa we were invited onto the lake to christen the new fishing nets. Cheers echoed across Karago as I stood up in the hand carved boat in an attempt to caste the first new net – nearly following it into the water! A present of one of several fish caught that morning was gratefully accepted but, even though wrapped in several layers of banana leaves, I had visions of it pre-empting me into my hut that night. The temperature was in the high eighties.

More singing, dancing and waving saw us on the road once more until the Gasiza women were mere hazy, bobbing specks in the distance.

Finally reaching the mountain market we parked our vehicle; no way could we continue other than on foot. From then on it was a continuous steady, but arduous climb during which we met barefoot children who eased bundles of sticks from shaven heads so that they could give us a hug; muscular young men, on their way to market, leaned backwards and discharged their massive sacks of potatoes onto the ground in order to greet us.

I found the climb tiring and difficult; I had been out of Ruhengeri hospital only three weeks since an attack of malaria; even with a boy from the market to carry my back pack I needed to rest every half hour. My T-shirt was soon soaked in sweat and my water supply low. Rwandans have no alternative but to walk, climb, carry and endure disease on a daily basis I, at least, only have to suffer occasionally.

We attracted a retinue of adults and children while passing thatched huts dotted about on the terraced mountainside. Men and women rested and waved from a distance before they continued swinging their hoes or bent again to tend their crops. It soon became obvious Mzungus were not often seen on these mountains

Near the summit we were asked to visit a home in which they had a new baby boy - born during the night. As I entered the small compound outside the hut the mother was preparing the afterbirth for a ritual - or consuming. I didn't ask any questions but concentrated on the bundle lying in a hand woven basket on the baked earth. It was wrapped in a clean piece of white cloth, its eyes were closed and the remains of its latest meal remained congealed around its rose bud mouth. Fortunately, at this altitude flies are not such a problem.

After showing me the baby, naked apart from a small pad of

material under its bottom, the mother strapped it to her back in the usual fashion and accompanied us ready to return to the fields. I was concerned for a long cord was still attached and its belly button protruded ominously.

Suddenly a horde of mountain dwellers descended from above and we were finally with the Batwa.

The welcome was startling for the crowd seemed to come from nowhere and burst into song, intermingled with clapping and dancing, as soon as they saw us. I was told they rarely had visitors and never Mzungus.

I expected them all to be pygmies but many were of reasonable height due to intermarriage. Nevertheless they were some of the poorest people I had encountered so far in Rwanda.

A haggard pygmy of questionable age came towards me wearing a long coat reaching to his bare feet. His gnarled fingers plucked at five wires stretched over, and secured to, an empty, rusty, oblong tin and several harsh, high pitched twangs emanated from this homemade instrument as he lifted one foot and then the other in time with his orchestrations. Behind him was his home, built like a tiny igloo made of straw and just about large enough for two small people to sleep in foetal fashion. The sole item of furniture was a car tyre near the entrance which held a small, round tin in its rim. This, I was informed, was his night light. I am unable to explain how it worked for there was nothing in the tin apart from a piece of thick string and I can only presume he poured an ignitable substance into the tin and lit the string.

I had brought several presents with me and rummaged in my back pack to see if there was anything suitable for my musician, unfortunately no guitar or piano, but a brightly coloured T-shirt emerged. He moved forward, put out his hands, then pointed to his chest. Before I could place the shirt into his hands his coat was stripped off and I was confronted with a bare chest; he wore only a pair of ragged trousers under the coat. He donned the shirt, continually plucking at it in time with the clapping and singing from the surrounding onlookers and, although cold at this altitude, his coat was thrown into the straw igloo and he proceeded to show off his new attire to all in the vicinity. Had it been the crown jewels he couldn't have been more delighted.

Continuing our tour of the Batwa commune I was anxious to know if the children went to school, if so, where? Where was their water supply? What happened if they were ill?

Stoically I was informed, 'Children don't go to school because there's no school they can walk to.'

'We get water by going down the mountain and collecting it from the river at the bottom.' (It had taken me three and a half hours to reach the summit!)

'If we're ill we either live or we die, it is God's will!'

Lying out in the open behind one of the huts I could see a girl curled up on a few strands of straw. Her eyes were closed and she didn't move as we approached her bed, I was told she had been put outside because she was, 'Very hot.'

I knelt down and felt her forehead, it was burning and beads of perspiration trickled down the side of her face. I felt sure she was suffering from malaria.

I found a packet of paracetamol in my kit and poured a little of the water from my bottle into a plastic mug the mother produced. Together we lifted the girl into a sitting position and managed to get her to drink but she couldn't swallow the tablets. Finally I decided to crush them and stir them into the water, in this way they were administered. The mother shook my hands and then kissed both the palms whilst a silent crowd gathered and watched from a respectful distance.

I left what remained of my boiled water and four further tablets. Francois explained to the mother that she must make sure the daughter drank plenty of boiled water, while her temperature was so high, to avoid dehydration. I'm sure the mother had no idea what dehydration meant but she nodded - we hoped.

Our departure took longer than expected for no one would let me leave without shaking hands. We arranged to take one of the Batwa teenage boys with us as we would be passing the Ruhengeri hospital on our return and I decided to try and obtain something to help the sick girl.

After a three hour wait at the hospital - there were thirty two people in front of me - I was given two packets each containing six tablets for which I paid 6,000 Rwandan francs (approximately £6.00). A label was stuck onto the small transparent packets with only the following instructions -

On one packet was one vertical straight line together with a full sun, presumably one tablet to be taken during the day. On the other packet were two vertical straight lines and a crescent moon - presumably two tablets to be taken at night!

It was impossible for the Batwa boy to return to his people that day so he stayed the night with me and returned to the Twa the following morning. Goodness knows how long it took him or how many miles he had to walk. I gave him some francs in the hopes he would get a lift from someone.

Five weeks later I received news the girl had recovered, the musician was still wearing his T-shirt and the Batwa commune wanted to know when I was going to visit them again!

Chapter Twenty Two

'Fields have eyes and woods have ears'
John Haywood

Dusabe and My 'Little Old Man'

The half hour before dawn is always shrouded in mystery as the sleepy moon gradually retires to make way for the waking sun.

Although all seems still there is a suggestion of movement as wisps of wood smoke from an early breakfast fire, mingle with the gossamer mist rising from the dew-covered ground.

Myriads of stars still hold a little of their brightness, enhanced by the absence of pollution and dearth of domestic or commercial lights.

Sometimes I like to walk alone in the quiet, peaceful part of the forest where I can take refuge from the ugliness of genocide, war and poverty for a short period before the demands of the day begin.

Strolling in flip-flops the cold earth rejuvenates my tired old feet and I savour the damp, misty morning caresses which smooth and cool my sun burnt arms and face.

I think of the poor impoverished souls who possibly died at this hour, on this same path, during the genocide and war years. It proves a sobering thought and, with the peace that now surrounds me, difficult to envisage the Machiavellian workings and terrible cruelty committed by one human being against another which led to the massacre and exodus of thousands of Rwandans from their homeland before, during and after the genocide.

The few wild animals remaining in Rwanda, apart from the mountain gorillas and their cohabiting friends the golden monkeys, are the black and white colobus and chimpanzees at Nyungwe Forest and a selection of plain's animals at Akagera National Park. Fortunately a profusion of beautiful birds can still be seen and heard in the foothills of the Virungas.

I'm not usually alone for long on my morning walk. As the chilled earth waits patiently for the morning sun a little girl realises I sometimes rise early and so makes sure she is ready for me when I reach a certain spot, some distance from the main village, where her hut is tucked away. Dusabe runs to greet me barefoot, pitifully thin and wearing a faded, ill fitting dress; she has grown very little in the eight months since I was last in Rwanda. Her cold little hand finds mine as she jabbers away quietly in Kinyarwanda, sometimes in a whisper for she doesn't want anyone to hear us and share our magic moments together.

She likes to wear my small LED wrist torch and flash it around searching for scurrying bijou creatures escaping from the monsters invading their territory at such an ungodly hour.

As the moon's pale shards slither through the trees' waking limbs, like shoals of silver fish, Dusabe attempts to capture them with her nimble frog-like jumps and forgets her previous intentions of silence. These are serendipity moments

Each time we near the trees in the foothills her little hand pulls at mine warning me it is time to return for the forest, I'm told, harbours wild dogs and other demons. I sense the fear the child experiences as her fingers clench tightly round mine. We stop for a minute or two during which I hear a sharp, explosive bark in the distant foothills but I assure her it's too far away to be of danger to us. Nevertheless she turns me around and pulls in the direction of the village, so I finally submit - who am I to say the only inhabitants of the forest are birds and friendly little creatures?

On our return journey the moon diminishes into a ghostly spectre high in the sky. Dawn greets us and we are able to gather and munch bunches of a plant whose stalks are topped with four large, dark green leaves similar in shape to a four leafed clover and tasting a little like aniseed. Breakfast may also include stolen, various coloured, raw beans picked and popped from their pods. Dusabe giggles as I toss the beans into the air, throw back my head, and endeavour to catch them in a gaping mouth. I then aim them at her mouth which she often closes in order that I miss the target.

By the time we near the village it's awake and we meet women making for the fields with hoes slung across their shoulders and babies strapped to their backs. Older children chat as they balance large empty water carriers on shaven heads, followed by three and four year olds who will struggle with the weight of their smaller containers during their return journey from wherever water is obtainable.

Dusabe puts her arms around me for a hug before she skips off to her hut and I return to prepare for yet another warm day. There are no long hours of ennui in my life when in Rwanda and, as I near the commune, I see Patchy Patchy with yet another bloody wound; a mother with a crying baby; a child with a cut above her right eye, all waiting for my attention.

I attend to as many minor ailments as possible. These can be anything from earache, stomach ache, boils, diarrhoea, festering wounds, worms or just plain hunger. On this particular morning the only solution is to administer paracetamol to an elderly women, suffering from aching, rotting teeth, who becomes extremely agitated when I inform her I'm unable to extract the offending, crumbling, black molars.

'Surgery' finished I gather my medical kit together and, on turning round, notice a small child making his way towards me, both hands endeavouring to keep an ill fitting pair of trousers from descending. His trouser legs are made of differing material and are not stitched together so one has an occasional preview of skinny buttocks from the rear and a little willy from the front!

Most days he plods along on tiny, mud-caked, flat feet, his thin arms usually dangling beside short bowed legs; large mucus filled eyes stare from an oversized head. I've never heard him speak and he ignores the other children - he lives in a world of his own.

Occasionally I find it hard to deal with some of the requests for help. Lack of clean water and nutritious food creates many health problems such as suppurating head sores in children, the head of this sorrowful 'little old man' of about three years of age being a prime example.

He has no objection to me taking him by the hand and leading him to where I have scissors, surgical gloves, shampoo and a bowl of water. The heads of most children are shaved to prevent lice but matted, foul smelling tufts have been left on my little old man's head and festering sores have formed. I cut the tufts of hair as short as possible, gently bend his little body over the cold water and begin shampooing in an effort to reach the source of just one of his many problems.

He makes no sound as my determined fingers vigorously massage the infected areas. His knees sag so I stop to rest his bent little body and begin again only when he initiates the procedure by pressing his thumb against mine. Blood runs as scabs and puss are removed so I wrap his head in a clean piece of cloth while I throw away the obnoxious contents of the bowl, wipe it clean and refill it, before I commence the elimination of the remaining hair and scabs.

The sun is warm so I sit with him for a while and allow the healing rays to work a little of their magic. Once dry I treat the scabs with antiseptic cream before cleaning out his ears with cotton buds and wiping the continuous flow of snot from his nose. He cups his tiny hands together and waits for the inevitable special treat - two bonbons.

I take his hand and walk with him to my hut where I have emergency clothing and there find a pair of shorts for him to wear while I deal with, and restyle, his ill fitting garments. On turning them inside out I find the seams are alive with lice so call two of the girls over to remove the invading horrors - the girls are extremely adept at pinching and dispatching lice between their thumb nails.

I wash the garments, sew them together, cut both legs to the same length then realise the waist is far too big. Remembering the girls' dresses secreted in my hold all have a half tie belt, I remove two lengths and make a rather pretty flowered belt for the now restyled, clean, lice free trousers.

My 'little old man' now saunters jauntily through the village, arms swinging smartly at his sides, turning his badly scared, shiny head right and left in the hopes everyone is looking at him now he has hand stitched Savile Row trousers.

I'm not sure what happened to the big toe on his left foot but the nail is decidedly disfigured as is the end of the toe. I presume it has been squashed at some time with a heavy object.

He doesn't know how to hold a crayon or remove the paper from a bonbon but I think it's time we taught him now he has his new outfit.

After 'surgery' I take a meander through the village greeting everyone with 'Mwaramutse' and 'Amakuru' and visit my favourite little Rwandan, Pinky-Perky (nickname). He's recovering from an attack of malaria so I make sure he has enough boiled water to drink and the bowl outside his door is full ready for all to wash their hands after going to the toilet.

Chapter Twenty Three

'Once Seen, Never Forgotten!'

Urgent Visits

Adaptability regarding one's attitude towards going to, and using, the toilet is an absolute necessity when visiting many parts of Africa - Rwanda being no exception - and it was on this hot and unusually humid day I learned what 'a trip to the corn' meant.

My two litre bottle of water was empty before noon which meant I needed to wee ..... and urgently, by one o'clock.

With wide eyed children, as usual, watching my every move I surreptitiously checked for the essential small pad of English toilet paper stored in my backpack. On the occasions when it has been necessary to use various leaves the immediate, and after affects had not been exceptionally pleasant.

Swinging my pack over one shoulder I set off in anticipation of finding a quiet spot but, unfortunately with at least a dozen imps skipping along beside me all wanting to hold my hand, I was at a loss what to do for by this time I was bursting.

A Kinyarwanda word for 'stay here' suddenly came to mind and with an authoritative intonation I shouted 'Gumaho.' It must have been correct for it worked! With a look of utter surprise everyone stopped dead. I accentuated this command by holding up both hands, palms facing out.

The walk began again with a game resembling 'What's the Time Mr Wolf?' for I could see several children move quickly forward a few steps each time I turned around. The gap between us widened so I darted into a field of maize hoping to lose the stalkers. After a few minutes I was sure I had succeeded. I stood erect listening for any sound but all was quiet; hurriedly I undid the button and zip on my trousers, bent my knees and bared all.

Within seconds the tall maize stems surrounding me parted near the ground and a multitude of grinning, black faces peered from between them; I was totally surrounded with an audience of children. I had no alternative but to finish that which I had started, before standing up and heaving the trousers into position. Immediately I stood up the faces disappeared as if by magic - as silently as they had appeared.

I recounted this story to my foreman who laughingly said, 'That's what we call 'a trip to the corn' but we don't usually have an audience.'

-- ooo0ooo –

When helping the Red Cross on Nkombo Island after the earthquake in Cyungugu, a soldier escorted me to the village latrine. It was the usual mud, sand and wood variety with no windows and a door that refused to close. Inside I noticed two large bricks concreted either side of the inevitable 'hole.'

A good contortionist's act would have been hard pressed to better the entertainment which followed. With an outstretched arm I held the door closed with one hand whilst undoing my trouser button and zip with the other. The trick was to keep the bottom of my trousers from touching the unsavoury floor, after all this was the village communal! The only light came through narrow cracks in the door or when it opened during my fluctuating contortions.

It was difficult to place both feet squarely on the uneven bricks, so difficult in fact my right ankle keeled over and my right foot, leg and trousers proceeded rapidly down the 'hole.'   I reeled back against the wall and the door flew open! Luckily my guard was standing with his back to the toilet, hands on hips and legs akimbo, so I was not centre stage.

The state of my attire left much to be desired, one boot having reached the contents residing at the bottom of 'the hole' and a trouser leg that now sported liquid browns and khaki and an odour which was definitely not Chanel Number Five. I composed myself as well as could be expected in the circumstances.

The door was still wide open as I completed my toiletries, pulled up, buttoned and zipped my trousers and made a quick exit. After taking off my boot and emptying the evil smelling sludge I kept a reasonable distance from my guard - for obvious reasons.

By the time we left the island late that night the aroma was pretty pungent and my colleagues took great delight in telling me so.

---ooo0ooo---

Being privileged to share the use of a flush toilet (not en-suite) in a small hotel, when staying two nights in Kigali, resulted in chaos and not the luxury I anticipated. I nearly died of a heart attack several times during the first night when a steam train passed only metres from my door, its imminent entry heralded by a triumphant trombone with earthquake qualities. I decided action was needed before retiring for the second night if the flush toilet was to stay in use.

I also suffered a further problem. Each time one struggled to sit down on the toilet seat, manufactured of pitted, black, cheap plastic, the lid possessed the capacity for snapping shut and trapping whatever clothing or bare flesh was in the vicinity. To remedy this took only a few minutes and, as the string ensnaring this 'Venus Fly Trap' remained in situ, I presumed the other guests found the remedy acceptable.

Unfortunately, I left my treasured toilet roll on the cistern after a late night visit and it had, of course, disappeared by morning. This really was a serious loss.

The following night with ear plugs at the ready, a notice saying, 'PLEASE DO NOT FLUSH THIS TOILET AFTER MIDNIGHT' hung on the outside handle of the toilet door and a note inside saying, 'PLEASE RETURN MY TOILET ROLL' I retired about 11.30pm.

It worked and I slept the sleep of the dead until about 6.00am. Unfortunately the toilet roll was not returned, it was probably wending its way into the depths of central Rwanda or residing beside a 'hole' in Cyungugu.

Chapter Twenty Four

*'Both tears and sweat are salty, but they render a different result.
Tears will get you sympathy; sweat will get you change'.*

Jesse Jackson

Cyungugu

After leaving Gregorie Kibanda Airport I was to make my way to
Cyangugu a town 5-6 hours away to south west of Rwanda, near
the shores of Lake Kivu and only a half a kilometre from the
Democratic Republic of the Congo border. I had received a request
from the Bishop of Cyangugu to build a water tank for a school
desperate for water.

A taxi of dubious vintage took me to the centre of the bustling,
dusty capital Kigali where most of the buses left for various parts
of the country. There were three main roads out of Kigali, one east,
connecting to Akagera Game Park, one north west to Ruhengeri,
the third south west leading to Cyangugu; I was to take the long
tortuous journey south west to Cyangugu.

I was dropped at a heaving bus rank in the capital but not,
unfortunately, one with transport for Cyangugu. The necessary
bus proved to be in another street five hundred yards away with the
consequence I had to haul two hold alls and backpack to the desired
destination.

After questioning several people I found my bus. This should have
seated twelve people but already held fourteen, plus the driver, and all
the seats were full apart from two small, hard fold-up contraptions.
Try as we may we could not fit both my hold alls into the boot of the
vehicle and there was no roof rack. Fortunately the man sitting on
my left in a reasonably comfortable seat, was unperturbed at having
one of my hold alls overlapping his knees, I just hoped he realised it
would be there for the next five hours unless he was alighting en
route, in which case I would slide into his seat before anyone else did!

We stopped only for road blocks in the mountains, of which there
were many, due to insurgents who continually worried the area.
Most of the journey was a blur and I managed to catch only glimpses
of the beautiful, terraced, mountainous countryside while travelling

at 90 kph. The vehicle swayed carelessly right and left at each bend but I experienced minimal movement; we were packed together as tightly as sardines. My knees were continually bruised by the seat in front; both shoulders were in close contact with neighbouring passengers and most of my 23 kg hold all was on my lap.

At some hair-raising bends, known well by the driver, we had to almost stop and it was close to one of these, nearing the half way mark to Cyangugu, a band of rough looking individuals jumped down onto the road from the mountain on our left. Although still on the bend our driver put his foot hard down on the accelerator and drove straight at them then, swerving his steering wheel hard over at the last minute, returned the vehicle to its original route. I was later informed a gun had been brandished but all I experienced was several bumps and thuds as the bus veered to the edge of a sixty foot drop scattering the thugs en route. There was no stopping to see if anyone had been injured when we were once again on the straight and narrow and our nonchalant driver turned round, displaying a grin from ear to ear, when a crescendo of cheering and clapping erupted from the passengers.

At the next army checkpoint our driver reported the incident and one of the soldiers said a few words into his walkie-talkie then proceeded to squeeze in, with a machine gun over his shoulder, and accompany us to the next checkpoint. On leaving the bus he cheerily waved us goodbye shouting, 'Be careful, but drive fast.'

On alighting from the bus in Cyangugu we were informed there were two bullet holes in the rear boot door these, luckily, having embedded themselves into someone's rolled up mattress.

Charles, the Bishop's tall, serious faced personal assistant, met me with a dilapidated taxi for which I paid. The next two days were spent at a newly erected guest house surrounded by attractive, newly laid out gardens and thatched rondavels on the shores of Lake Kivu. This proved to be a comfortable, clean abode belonging to the Anglican Diocese and sported beautiful views over the lake to the DRC and its majestic mountains. The town of Bukavu and the Custom's Post between Rwanda and the DRC being only a stone's throw away.

I had just time to drop my luggage into a clean, sunlit room and run to a (very quiet) en suite **flush** toilet before two very friendly

Rwandan chambermaids came through the open door and wanted to know all about England, what was I doing in Rwanda and would I teach them English.

I suggested they came along the next day when I would begin tuition and tell them, in my halting French, as much as I could about the UK.

Sure enough they returned during their break about 10am the following morning and entered holding, by the tail, what I first thought was a white mouse.

The taller of the two girls waggled the 'creature' before me and said, 'Qu'est-ce que c'est?'

On closer inspection I found it was a clean, unused tampon. The cotton wool had been pulled from the white tubular container by its long white string, and was now being shaken between an inquisitive finger and thumb. Presumably it had been found under the bed in one of the new rondavels occupied previously by a German family.

Many Rwandans speak French as well as Kinyarwanda so as yet, with only half a dozen words of Kinyarwanda in my vocabulary and limited French, I endeavoured to explain the use of this fluffy white item. There were looks of wide eyed amazement, giggles and eventually nods of understanding, before the girls left with 'the mouse' still dangling between thumb and forefinger. They returned late that afternoon for their English lessons – minus mouse!

On the afternoon of the third day I was finally ferried to what was to be my home for the next six weeks, a two roomed, brick built dwelling with a small garden containing lime and avocado trees and magnificent views over Lake Kivu stretching to the mountains of the Democratic Republic of the Congo.

I was to work on a thirty two cubic metre water tank for a small Anglican school which consisted of three brick built school rooms, on an elevated piece of land, about a two kilometres from the town and just a short distance from the Bishop's house. There was water in the vicinity but it was too expensive for the school to purchase; the tank was to provide reasonable clean drinking water and enough to clean toilets (concrete holes in the floor) and classrooms.

Much the same as my first tank in Ruhengeri this one was to be built of brick and local stone, adjacent to one of the school's classrooms which sported a corrugated roof. Guttering was fixed just below this roof together with a pipe which extended from the guttering into the tank. Each time it rained water flowed from the roof, through the pipe and, into the tank. Also fitted at appropriate points on the tank was an overflow pipe and tap. The tank was to be used by the school in term time and the indigenous population during holidays.

We commenced the project after my two day's rest; Charles recruited my workforce plus a tall, slim Rwandan foreman called Francois with a charming smile. It looked as though I was to be lucky again with a good looking foreman, my first one at Imbaraga had been a dead ringer for Clarke Gable. (The older generation will remember him in the film 'Gone with the Wind')

The men were all raring to go but eyed me with suspicion and apprehension, as had the gang in Ruhengeri initially but, after I spent five days sitting on a pile of second-hand rocks cleaning them with a viscous looking machete - they were so much cheaper than new ones - I was soon part of the team. My other duties included purchasing materials, carrying bricks and mixing cement, helping to keep bricklayers supplied and also paying the wages at the end of the week.

Our hods consisted of half a ragged edged, five litre plastic container, a bucket with a hole in it, a battered dustbin lid and a couple of sacks for transporting the sand and gravel. Unfortunately the ancient lorry, which we were very lucky to purloin, was unable to get onto the site due to a one in four gradient. Loaded, it would have managed the down-hill section without any problems but the suspect brakes left me with visions of it continuing through the school buildings!

I removed my wedding ring after a couple of days, even through work gloves it was getting scratched. My hands gradually turned into grappling irons and my arms bore scars from cuts and grazes for several weeks. The men soon noticed my wedding ring was no longer on my finger and I was asked to give a reason. I told them it was getting damaged, I didn't want any of them getting ideas, although at my age I don't think I need have worried.

It was hot most mornings by eight o'clock and appallingly wet, for a very short period, most afternoons. The men knew exactly when to expect rain, I think they could smell it coming. Empty cement bags were gathered together in readiness to cover the mixed cement and partly completed brickwork.

Unfortunately we had to fell some trees to construct ladders and scaffolding, but much of the wood could be used again and I made a patchwork kennel for a stray puppy, called Boz, with the leftovers.

The work progressed well and at intervals during the day I was introduced to the genitalia of the oldest man in our team, each time he bent down you could see everything he owned. He didn't seem to worry, so neither did I, but I did present him with a pair of my trousers on finishing the project for which he was delighted.

This same gnome-like, elderly gentleman whom I called Pop, began to sag at the knees as he tried to carry, on his head, stones weighing up to fifteen kilograms and more. A young boy would heave them up, without too much difficulty, and place them on the old man's ingata (thick ring made of banana fronds) which protected his head. Immediately my gnome's stature diminished to half its normal size. The boy would then endeavour to pull Pop up by his arms, in order to straighten his knees, before he staggered down the slope and released his cargo with a huge gasp of relief. After gaining his breath, and retrieving his ingata, he repeated this hourly toil to keep the bricklayers supplied. I felt sure he would drop down dead if I did nothing to alleviate this slave labour and, not wanting his death on my conscience, I diplomatically asked the foreman if he could lighten the old man's load without drawing too much attention to the fact. My request was granted; Pop's knees - and heart - lasted at least for the duration of my stay.

We completed the task in just under six weeks with the aid of these eight very black, very often shoeless, young and old, artistic, hardworking, friendly Rwandans.

Being just south of the equator dawn seeped through every morning about 5.30am and the team, after having sometimes walked many kilometres, began work at 7.30am until between 4 and 5pm with only a half an hour's break at noon. There were no tea breaks or smokes just an occasional drink of water. I had a two hour break at lunchtime but soon discovered several of the men had nothing to eat all day so I returned about two o'clock with anything from boiled eggs to a saucepan full of rice. All were gratefully received and disappeared within minutes! I had a small, wooden, home-made solar oven with me and used it daily placing either pasta, vegetables or rice inside before leaving for work each morning and, voila! lunch was ready by about twelve noon.

It was a sad day when Francois' youngest child was run over by a lorry. There were, of course, no apologies or compensation. He had only two days off from work, the day of the accident and the day of the funeral. I attended the funeral but kept to the perimeter of the mourners. It was such a tiny, homemade, rough wooden coffin. There were no flowers just stones placed over a patch of ground measuring roughly a metre by half a metre.

Most of my evenings were spent with dear little Boz, a five week old puppy, thrown out because she was a bitch.

One Saturday morning, on my way to market, I heard a faint whimper coming from a ditch. I'm deaf in my left ear so swivelled my head, as one would an aerial to obtain better reception, and finally honed in on a section of ditch a few feet behind me. There I found a wet, bedraggled, thin and very poorly little Boz - a bitch puppy. I didn't continue to market that Saturday, instead I stuffed Boz under my poncho and returned 'home.'

Warm water was the order of the day and within an hour Boz was bathed and de-loused and didn't take much tempting to swallow a few spoons full of warm dried milk then, wrapped cosily in my fleece, she slept for the next two hours. Boz reminded me of a young child who can be dying one minute and turning summersaults on its bed the next, for when she awoke she immediately tottered over to where I was sitting and, with big appealing eyes, looked up into mine saying, 'How about some more food?'

With TLC Boz was soon a beautiful roly-poly bundle of fun and a wonderful companion to me especially over the Christmas period. She liked anything especially rice, vegetables, bananas, mangoes - and toes, the latter were always readily available for none of the children wore shoes.

On Christmas Eve Boz and I shared a massive tilapia fish caught in the lake. This I dissected with my fingers - it's a very bony fish - then proceeded to munch a mouthful myself and give a smaller portion to Boz.

I sat enthralled by the spectacular storm emanating from behind the mountains in the DRC. The sheet and fork lightening lit the roof of the sky as it streaked through the angry, quick moving clouds; the ground grumbling as the thunder echoed across lake Kivu. Boz, now full of tilapia, snuggled under my woollen jersey with an occasional whimper and snuffled her wet, button black nose into my neck surfacing only when the storm abated and she was ready for more tilapia and milk.

Regardless of weather conditions pollution was negligible and Lake Kivu at night mirrored the sky above. The eternal Milky Way mingled with dozens of diminutive, dancing lights attached to miniature fishing boats which rocked gently as nets were adroitly thrown into the lake trapping tilapia and other unsuspecting fish ready for an early morning market.

The market was almost an hour's walk away (each Saturday) when dry, but negotiating some of the one-in-three short, sharp undulating and pitted clay inclines became more and more difficult when it rained and resulted in a strenuous three hour round trip. Clay gradually built up on the soles of one's boots forming lead weights and, with a fully laden back pack, made climbing K2 look easy! On one occasion I fell backwards and slid precariously down the bumpy, red clay slope taking several other people with me. Luckily I was un-laden as I was going to, not coming from, the market.

I will not linger on my visit to the butcher's open stall, intending to purchase meat for Boz, it was too nauseating, but will mention the fact that I was very nearly mobbed by several women from the DRC one day when endeavouring to photograph one of steep inclines I had to negotiate if I wanted food for the next week. The Congolese women, unfortunately, would have been in the background and I didn't wait to find out if they wanted money or whether it was against their culture or religion to have photographs taken. It was perfectly obvious they were not pleased about something so I beat a hasty retreat.

There were five or six of them and, although small in stature, their strength was something to be respected. They walk barefoot from the mountains in the DRC, over the border to Cyangugu, a journey of at least thirty kilometres. They return home fully laden with heavy sacks on their backs which are supported by a broad band of cloth extending round the bottom of their load and up around their foreheads, the head and neck taking all the strain. Sometimes six or eight chickens are also carried, either by their legs, or stuffed into any available orifice, the poor creatures' mouths wide open as they gasp for air and water. Unfortunately I never did get the photo I wanted, it was either raining or too many women from the DRC were in the vicinity!

I had never experienced an earthquake until ten past eleven one Sunday morning the earth began to grumble and shake. Boz, David - Charles's youngest boy - and I were playing football. Even Boz must have experienced a sensation for she stopped playing and ran under a bush. David ran to me and I put my arms around him whilst looking down the slope to Lake Kivu.

Near the lake's shore was a Catholic church with a peculiar flat roof onto which had been built a half circle, brick wall about three metres high. I watched a crack appear and then the bricks began to disintegrate and smash to the ground. The earth trembled beneath our feet and we could hear glass smashing and screams. David buried his head into my body and tightened his little arms around me while I could do nothing but stand and wonder what would happen next having seen on TV the damage and gaping cracks earthquakes had made in other countries.

After what seemed like many minutes but was, I understand only seconds, the earth stopped moving. I picked up Boz, took David's hand and made for David's home a short distance away.

'Il est un trembelement de terre,' shouted David's father as he ran towards us.

The town of Cyangugu had suffered badly. A church, full of morning worshipers, had collapsed completely trapping and killing people. Part of the hospital's maternity ward had been destroyed together with several schools. Luckily, being a Sunday, the schools were empty. Many brick and rukarakara homes were either badly damaged or completely demolished. Even the prison on the outskirts of the town had not escaped the earthquake's fury. Fortunately the crack in the earth, near to where I was staying, was small but, nevertheless, frightening to see.

The Government brought in helicopters to take many of the wounded to Kigali, Cyungugu hospital being unable to cope, but it was five days before assistance arrived from other organisations the first being from the Red Cross.

Minor tremors continued throughout the day and for the next

fortnight, and people were afraid to go near any substantial structures built of brick or sandstone. Early on Monday morning Charles and I made our way to the hospital and I went immediately to the children's ward where I found severely wounded children lying on the concrete floor and a dearth of blankets, food and mattresses.

One must depend on friends or relatives for food and sheets etc., when in most rural African hospitals and Cyangugu was no exception.

I asked a doctor if there was any mode of transport available in order I may try to get into to the town and procure food and other essentials. He found me an ambulance and driver and we made our way passing hundreds of dazed people, with their belongings, too afraid to stay inside.

There were mounds of rubble everywhere, half buildings and cracked walls. The Bcr bank had been undergoing extensive renovations and a second storey added - it now sported just a damaged single storey surrounded by bricks and mortar.

We parked the ambulance and went in search of maize flour, rice, mattresses and blankets all which we finally found, together with a small bag of sugar and some packets of biscuits. The rice we had to scoop up from the floor with our hands picking out bits of rubble as we tipped it back into ripped sacks. I think others had been there before us!

I spent the next three days helping with the children, feeding those unable to feed themselves and generally endeavouring to make their lives a little more comfortable with a mattress instead of cold concrete and a warm blanket for night time. Several, who were well enough, enjoyed crayoning and all wanted their photographs taken; the inscriptions and drawings I added to plaster casts were in great demand. One young girl, who lay completely naked on a plastic mattress, was delighted with my T-shirt and knickers and refused to wear the childrens' clothes I finally obtained for her from the market. Her wounds were severe and her parents had died in the church.

With some cajoling I obtained several large silver sheets from the Red Cross for the prison, these proved ideal for protection while the buildings were being repaired.

Money from our Trust meant for a project in Kinigi, was spent in Cyungugu in the children's ward and building wooden dwellings for several local families who had lost their homes. The Kinigi project had to wait for another year.

Saturday was spent on Nkombo Island helping the Red Cross distribute rush mats and blankets. Our two lorries, loaded with aid, were parked on the edge of the river while their contents were loaded into three very large, but ancient, wooden boats carved by the people on the island. I and five others, two men and three women, were transported by the army in a rubber dingy with an outboard and arrived soaked to the skin; the sun was so hot it didn't take long for our clothes to steam and dry.

The chief and others in authority on the island were there to escort us to the centre of the village which, incidentally, was a twenty minute walk uphill passing many damaged and demolished dwellings en route including a school. The men of the village unloaded the boats and carried the goods to the village hall.

I presumed my companions had carried out such distributions in the past for there were hundreds of people milling round us with extended hands and I wondered how such crowds would be managed for, at one stage, they surged and we couldn't move.

It was frightening.

After pushing people out of the way we struggled to the village hall and set about making up separate packs each containing either four, five or six sets of essentials. The chief and his colleagues were extremely organised and had lists which separated people into family groups and so, after two hours, the distribution began.

Names were called, a member of the family came forward and collected their appropriate pack, signed their name or made a thumb print, and retreated carrying their spoils on their head. Several very old women, without families, were unable to lift their pack and were helped by a member of another family.

Everything was very orderly, for most of the time, with spontaneous clapping breaking out as families walked down the line with their bundles. It wasn't until about two o'clock when a few disturbances broke out. Families at the end of the queue thought we were running out of blankets and began to break ranks. We immediately assured them by bringing out a further stock from the village hall and, thankfully, peace reigned until an easel clattered down onto the concrete outside the hall. Everyone tried to run away, many screaming, some falling down and being trampled upon in the rush to leave the area. They thought there was another earthquake - the majority slowly returning when they were assured all was well.

Towards 4pm our work was nearing completion when a string of village men arrived carrying long, large white nylon sacks, so heavy it needed two men to a sack. UNICEF was printed on the side of each sack. They were full of tin plates, cups, saucepans and bowls. I had been hoping it would be food as had the villagers, they didn't use tin cups and plates they carved and made their own from trees and fronds. I thought at the time how necessary it was to make sure the true necessities of life were delivered in times of emergency and not items thought up by an official behind a desk thousand of miles away.

We finally wended our way back to the rubber dingy as dusk descended and reached the other side of the river only to find one of the lorries had made its way down the bank into the river! It was either a case of another set of worn out brakes or someone had failed to leave the vehicle in gear and pull up the hand brake to its limit. We could do nothing to retrieve the vehicle for it was dark and we had no equipment with which to haul it out.

I was invited back to the hotel where a large contingent of the Red Cross were staying, and urged to stay and have a meal with them. What a spread! I felt extremely guilty for there was enough food to last me for six months. My clothes, and body odour, were still on the strong side after my experience with Nkombo's village toilet but, thankfully, I was able to wash before sitting down to eat with my companions

I was invited out to four meals while in Cyangugu, once by the English attaché visiting the area from the embassy in Kigali; to dinner with the Bishop and his family; by Charles' family on Christmas Day and by the Anglican Bishop's personal assistant upon the completion of the school's water tank.

The attaché was staying at the same rest house as the 'white mouse' and in which I had stayed eight weeks earlier. I was collected by the attaché himself, a seasoned looking gentleman of about fifty years of age; our transport was an elderly but well kept car which arrived promptly at 4pm. We enjoyed a most interesting repast and entertaining couple of hours for the attaché had been stationed in several embassies throughout the world, including Indonesia, so we had much in common to talk about.

Unfortunately, it began raining before we finished our meal of the inevitable boiled potatoes, oily cabbage, onions and tough, scraggy chicken. I politely ate a little of the chicken and then tried to hide the remainder under my fork, knife and halved paper serviette.

I could only be transported part of the way home because of the car getting stuck in mud on a steep incline. My attaché had to reverse, precariously, back down the slope while I was up to my ankles in mud as soon as I alighted from the car. I removed my well worn flip flops and continued to climb, barefoot, arriving home mud splattered and soaked to the skin to be warmly greeted by Boz who had found some of my clothes and made a nest for herself in my absence and also deposited a few puddles.

My last supper proved most interesting for the eating place was only a short distance from the border crossing point to the DRC and within a stone's throw from the town of Bukavu.

We entered a clean, reasonably lit, empty room with whitish cloths on six tables; dubious loud music echoed throughout the building. Having chosen our table we sat down and a pleasant, wide eyed boy produced a menu but pointed out the items of food and drink they had available that evening. These consisted of soup (unnamed) omelettes, chicken, cabbage, chips, coca cola, lemonade and bottled beer. I chose omelette and lemonade; my two companions chose chicken, chips and coke. I felt a little concerned for we were asked to pay for the meal before it was served. My friends, seemingly unconcerned, produced the required amount of Rwandan francs so I ceased to worry.

Half an hour went by; three quarters of an hour; one and half hours; and then, after two hours, the meals were placed before us, adequate but nothing outstanding to warrant the waiting time.

I found out, during my journey home, the owner of the restaurant was bankrupt and after our meals were ordered his son dashed over the border to Bukavu, where food was cheaper than in Cyungugu and, with the recently acquired cash, purchased the vegetables and a live chicken; returned; killed; dressed and cooked the chicken and vegetables and, eventually, served us!

At least we knew the produce was fresh!

Two days before I left Cyangugu six people, waiting to be called as witnesses against incarcerated Interahamwe, were found with their throats cut, this episode re-igniting memories of the horrific slaughter that had taken place during the genocide which left many bones resting at the bottom of Lake Kivu - a lake so beautiful but holding such dark secrets.

I left early for my return to Imbaraga in the hopes of obtaining a good seat on the bus; I didn't fancy another six hour journey on a hard folding seat!

I was first to arrive at the bus stop so placed my back pack on the comfortable window seat next to the driver's, the best seat on the bus, and went into the shop to purchase my ticket. On returning to the bus my pack had been moved to another rear seat and a young policeman had taken mine, two other policemen sat behind him. I politely told him he was sitting in my seat. He just shook his head and went on talking to his colleagues. I returned to the ticket seller and told him my problem, he said there was nothing he could do they were the police and you didn't argue with them. I returned to the bus feeling more than a little annoyed. Opening the passenger door I tapped the policeman on the shoulder and said in the best French I could muster, 'Excuse me this is my seat. I am seventy five years of age and have been working extremely hard at St Matthew's School for the last six weeks to provide them with a water tank' - or words to that effect.

By this time I was finding it hard to muster enough French to admonish them further so just added, 'Allez!' To my complete surprise the young policeman slid from his seat and, with a charming smile said, ' I respect you Madam,' then joined his colleagues who both had broad grins stretched across their faces. I thanked them politely and fed them with biscuits and bonbons en route.

When relating this story to a friend at Urugaga they said I was lucky I didn't get hauled off to gaol - I'm sure they were only joking?

Chapter Twenty Five

*'When you get through something that doesn't kill you
it makes you stronger'*

A Burnt Hand

During the latter part of a long and tedious bus journey from Cyungugu, via Kigali, Ruhengeri to Urugaga, an extremely heavy storm turned the track to Imbaraga village into a quagmire. Thankfully the sun decided to re-appear as I turned off the road onto the track and steam rose from large puddles and rivulets as they escaped into the forest.

Black faces stared at the Mzungu and one little girl stopped dead in her tracks as though paralysed. I dropped my packs, spread my arms, and the dirty little bundle leapt into them as it screamed, 'Deli!' (Rwandans have difficulty in sounding the letter r). A musty, eucalyptus aroma reached my nostrils as the thin, mud-stained arms gripped me tightly around the neck and two spindly little legs rested lightly on my tired hip bones. Tears gushed as I swept her up and around until we both fell to the ground deliriously happy at being together again. Within minutes I must have resembled a muddied Pied Piper as children continued to emerge from the forest. By the time I reached the commune I had either cuddled, picked up, touched thumbs or shaken hands with nearly every adult and child in the village.

Before I unpacked I collected wood, found matches and, with difficulty because of the damp wood, made a fire to boil water while I rummaged through my kit to find medical supplies.

Jeannie, a little girl of six or seven years had burned her hand in a fire. She sat on the ground in front of me with her left arm extended the black, barbequed, offensive smelling little digits drooping. She reminded me of a puppy with a wounded paw. Large drops of clear liquid rolled along the bottom of her lids finally overflowing onto her dusty, tear-stained cheeks as she searched my face for a possible source of relief from her pain.

I had no way of getting her to hospital for treatment and there was no visiting doctor I could call so, with water boiled and the medical

127

kit held ready by one of the girls, extremely proud to have been chosen as my assistant nurse, and my indispensable book 'Where there is no doctor' open to the page on burns, the operation began.

Each morning at dawn Jeannie waited for me with her retinue of hungry, cold and sometimes very wet siblings, some so young they were hardly able to walk but determined to miss nothing. Their wobbly, rickety little legs sometimes buckled beneath them and they had to be scooped up by anyone who was prepared to administer help and stop their tears.

Naturally the villagers, especially the children, became extremely interested in everything I did so tending Jeannie's burn was no exception. Our close audience would not be moved so I drew a circle in the dirt and made it clear that no one was to enter the circle in which Jeannie and I sat. Some of the children sat cross legged on the ground and shuffled slowly and surreptitiously on their bottoms nearer the forbidden line, others stood with folded arms, while a few adults peered and chatted in the background. Bosco, an older boy, found a stick and kept the children at bay. I didn't admonish him for he was only tapping at toes when they extended into the circle.

Jeannie's single parent never accompanied her so we always began the proceedings by lighting the fire and, while waiting for the water to boil, we sat together with my arm around her skinny shoulders enjoying a sticky orange or lemon bonbon. These bonbons were nectar to a child who had never tasted anything so deliciously sweet apart from the occasional stick of sugar cane which had usually been sucked and chewed previously by a dozen others before passing her amazingly white teeth.

The fingers of Jeannie's left hand were black and bloated; the back of the hand, between knuckles and wrist, constantly suppurated and the skin was beginning to flake on the palm.

Warm, boiled water was applied to the bandages every other day to remove the dressing which stuck solidly to the extensive burns. This area oozed rainbow coloured puss as I held the little body tightly and whispered what I hoped were soothing sounds as the discoloured, smelly dressing was gradually eased from her tiny hand. This was so small it fitted easily into the palm of my hand.

After about ten days I felt a little time in the early morning sun and fresh air would help the healing process for the wounds were exuding very little liquid and I was able to keep most of the hand dry after dusting with a puff of antiseptic powder. Before beginning this daily ritual Jeannie and I found a quiet grassy spot away from the village and I taught her to draw and crayon while her burnt hand rested on my clean towel allowing the unpolluted breeze and nature to take its course. I cut a length from a sterilised stocking to cover her hand like a glove and this, together with a dressing, was changed every few days.

The children were amazed to see that Jeannie's hand had turned pink, but I assured them further skin would grow and it would be brown. Jeannie wanted it to stay pink - she wanted to look like Deli!

Unfortunately it took many days of cleansing, cutting away blackened dead skin and much tender loving care before her pain disappeared completely. Time proved a great healer and she regained mobility in both hand and fingers.

On my return visits to the village a scraggy little creature always comes running to me with hand held high and a smile that tells me all is well. Nevertheless , I was extremely concerned one day when I heard women in a village talking about Yusi.

Chapter Twenty Six

'Truth emerges more readily from error than from confusion'

Yusi

Yusi was another girl who gave me much concern for a while. A scraggy little nine (ish) year old; the middle child of a family of ten with a Princess Diana expression. Her chin rested nearly on her chest, her head tilted a little to the left and her massive brown eyes travelled upwards as she looked at me under long, curly, black lashes. Most Rwandan children have these enviably long lashes

No matter what time I rose when I was based at Imbaraga she was there, hungry and cold clothed in only a torn, dirty dress - usually one I had given her the previous year but still fitting her as she had grown very little. The mother was anxious to commence birth control for she was only about forty years of age but looked sixty.

Strolling through the village one Sunday morning I joined a group of women husking beans. By this time I could understand a little Kinyarwanda so always greeted the women with, 'Waramutse, amakuru?' (How are things, what is your news?) to which they usually responded, 'Ni meza.' (fine - good news).

With the niceties over I sat and endeavoured to understand their conversation and was aghast when I heard the name Yusi and the fact that there was going to be a killing that day!

My companions seemed unconcerned when I hastily tried to find out more about 'the killing' but, as I became more agitated, their laughter increased. I could glean nothing more from them due to my lack of competence with the language so had to wait for someone who could unravel the facts surrounding this possible murder!

It was several anxious hours before I saw Oscari wending his way up the track and I could reiterate the conversation I thought I had heard that morning and my fears concerning Yusi. I asked him to visit Yusi's hut and question her parents. A broad smile appeared on Oscari's face as we questioned Yusi's mother. Yusi, he told me, was Kinyarwanda for guinea pig and as they were prolific breeders some families could occasionally afford to purchase them to provide a little protein in their diets.

Only the day before I had been caressing three dear little black, brown and white fluffy creatures and thinking how wonderful it was to find a family able to afford pets for their children.

My Yusi was safe but, unfortunately, the three little guinea pigs weren't!! They went into the pot with potatoes and 'farty' beans during the next few days.

I had much to learn - and not only the language.

Chapter Twenty Seven

'An ant on the move does more than a dozing ox'
Lao-Tzu

Rwandan Transport

Anyone visiting this beautiful, mountainous country has much to learn. One needs a good sense of humour, an abundance of patience and the ability to adjust to using little water. It's also useful if one is slight of stature for there were many occasions when it was necessary to squeeze myself into extremely small spaces on buses, bicycle cross bars and between sacks of potatoes or sand loaded onto the rear of lorries.

Being a white, elderly but small, exploitative Mzungu I was invariably successful in obtaining a lift if I extended a hand, inclined my head and produced a sorrowful, tired expression while standing at the side of the road; a vehicle of some description would invariably appear and hoist me aboard.

Modes of transport consisted of:-

(a) The rear carrier or crossbar of a black upright bicycle - this mode of transport usually left a barbeque pattern on my posterior

(b) The tubular metal carrier on the rear of a motorbike in the pouring rain on a 12 kilometre stretch of road which had more potholes and boulder traps than I had bruises

(c) Lorries stuck together with black tape and usually loaded with either rocks, bricks, potatoes or sand – the latter being the most comfortable and safest

(d) The 'bus'

(e) Two feet

If possible I opted for the rear of a lorry for the cabs could be extremely dangerous. Electric wires dangled from every angle and the rusted floors became so hot the soles of one's feet actually scorched; a lively tap dance being necessary on a long journey.

On one occasion, whilst bouncing along with acrid smoke belching between my feet and ensconced in between the driver and his mate, I noticed an attempted roof repair with what resembled a flattened tin. Rescued, empty silver cans (cooking oil donated by USA) were put

132

to numerous good uses but this repair looked unsafe. Every pothole sent our heads upwards against the rusted roof where a jagged piece of metal pointed down towards the right hand side of the driver's head - and was extremely close to mine! It soon became obvious why he wore a stout leather hat pulled well down over his sweating features.

Sitting on top of a ton of sand or sacks of potatoes with ninety degrees of sun beating down and swirling dust clouds filling your nose, ears, eyes and any other orifice one might have exposed, is not ideal but certainly less tiring than having to walk back to the commune after a seven hour stint digging water pipe trenches.

A trip on a bicycle cross bar can be extremely interesting. On one occasion my 'chauffeur' and I struck up a firm friendship during the ensuing closeness and prolonged do-se-do of my bottom along the cross bar towards his bouncing body while rocketing over the pitted terrain. I'm sure it wasn't my sweet smelling, sweaty body that contributed to our camaraderie but the offer of a Sunday lunch, cooked on an open fire, which included a dessert of local fried bananas, dribbled with honey gathered from wild bees in the foothills of the Virunga mountains. Who could resist such an offer?

The owner of this ancient sit-up-and-beg, but exceptionally sturdy, black bicycle, was a teacher in Ruhengeri who travelled the twelve kilometres to and from his village daily. His downhill journey to Ruhengeri was quick and effortless, although precarious – the uphill return - murder! Two of his most important items were a tyre repair kit, zipped safely in his jacket pocket, and a large, shiny, well oiled bell positioned on his handlebars.

Punctures were a daily occurrence for all modes of transport using this road. From its commencement until the last few hundred yards it was an experience never to be forgotten. There were multitudes of varying sized, deep uninviting holes and stones gravitating from small pebbles to boulder proportions, strewn throughout its length. Added to which the daily horde of travellers, whose slow pace and even slower response to a bell or horn, made it a most interesting journey when using any mode of transport to, or from, Kinigi.

Most Rwandans think nothing of walking twelve to eighteen kilometres daily, bare foot and with a sack of potatoes or other equally heavy commodity on their heads. As the journey from Kinigi to Ruhengeri is all downhill these pedestrians can be as much a hazard as the unkempt road, hence the necessity for a trusty bell and good brakes.

Occasionally I caught 'The Bus' home which periodically trundled out of the market square billowing clouds of fumes into a previously unpolluted atmosphere - the market being about a three kilometre walk from my project base at that time. One could sometimes wait for over an hour because it only departed with a full complement. This proved a wonderfully friendly, social occasion; with eighteen passengers instead of the legal twelve on board one was able to get to know one another extremely well before the vehicle ground its bone shattering journey to town.

Periodically during the journey 'The Bus' would bounce to a shuddering halt when someone suddenly decided, a little late, they wished to alight with mountains of baggage which very often included a baby hidden under brightly coloured cotton material. This was swathed cleverly around the back of the disembarking mother then tied tightly around her waist and across the top shelf of her large mature bosom. Usually several passengers had to disembark, together with their accoutrements, before this procedure could take place which gave those remaining on the bus a chance to stand up, shuffle, change places and spread out before embarkation began.

On one occasion an elderly woman, accompanied by a young boy, was chattering away to me in Kinyarwanda. The boy stared at me wide eyed while the brown hen, tucked comfortably under his arm, conveyed the nonchalance of a seasoned traveller.

Unfortunately, my travelling companion decided I wasn't getting the gist of the conversation. In frustration she finally took out one of her ample bosoms, waggled it menacingly at me then at the boy. I tried to look intelligent but desperately needed help. Fortunately a woman sitting behind us spoke French and she decided to intervene before I was attacked with the mother's extremely large, lethal weapon. She explained this was the mother's way of informing me she had suckled the child and it was her son. (I was suitably prepared the next time it happened some days later in Ruhengeri market and was nonchalantly able to show the mother I was fully aware whose child she had beside her). After saying goodbye to the mother, her son, and stroking the head of the now observant chicken, I alighted from the bus and crossed the busy main street carefully observing the oncoming traffic; vehicles drive on the right hand side of the road in Rwanda.

My elderly, school-uniform-producing friend was in his usual place on the pavement working at his ancient but very productive, treadle sewing machine. His rugged but handsome face, topped with short silver hair, always breaks into a beaming smile when we meet. He raised his still agile body from the rickety wooden stool and held out his pink-palmed, welcoming hands. I extended mine and he placed a long lingering kiss on both of my palms. His head was bowed but his large, limpid brown eyes travelled upwards, found mine, and the warmth flowed between us. We chatted and, as I had already given him material purchased from the local market, I produced either written measurements or different lengths of string giving approximate chest, shoulder and length sizes necessary for him to complete his task. He sews all the uniforms for our orphans at school plus many others, as needs arise, on the condition he saves any oddments of material for me. The children take great delight in producing dolls from these remnants especially at Christmas.

With Christmas only a few weeks away thoughts of children, who are no longer with us, return - especially Alphonsine and her family.

Chapter Twenty Eight

For there is hope of a tree, if it be cut down,
that it will sprout again,
and that the tender branch there of will not cease.

Job XIV : VII

Alphonsine - Part 1

Alphonsine knew she was eleven because her mother told her so early one morning when waking her for school.

'To-day is your birth date and you may bring your friend home after school and I'll see if I can get some sugar cane as a special treat. Just be sure you both come straight home taking the route I showed you yesterday and let Sandrine's mother know she can stay with us for the night.'

This family, together with a thousand others, was aware of the unrest existing throughout Rwanda at that time but could do nothing about it but pray and endeavour to live life as normally as possible.

Alphonsine's mother, a tall, straight, attractive Tutsi of about thirty-four year's of age, stood two small bowls of cold water on rough wooden stools outside the door of their hut for Alphonsine and her two younger brothers to take their morning wash. They were short of water; for three days Vestine had been afraid to go to her usual watering place four kilometres away from the village after two drunken individuals had attacked her. Dark bruising and swellings showed on her pale brown arms where they had pulled her from one to the other and taken her battered old water container.

The boys, stripped down to their briefs, cupped their pink-palmed hands quickly in and out of the cold water and splashed it indiscriminately onto their laughing faces and young bodies; for privacy Alphonsine carried her bowl to the rear of the thatched hut. As usual all remaining water was poured into a large dried gourd to be used again for washing clothes or watering plants.

'Hurry children,' Vestine called. 'Your breakfast is ready and you don't want to be late for school.'

All but Hazika, the youngest, were now subdued as they put their hands together to give thanks for their food and pray the day would be free from hostility and conflict. He climbed onto his mother's lap, hugged her tightly and began to cry. Vestine cradled him as she had when he was a baby.

'You must be a big boy now and eat up your breakfast with your brother and sister, you don't want to miss school with a new teacher arriving to-day.'

Much of the usual breakfast of maize flour and water, into which the children had spooned the last of the sugar, was left in their wooden bowls for they all knew their mother was worried and none could eat much even though they knew they would be hungry later in the day.

Alphonsine shouldered the neatly sewn Hessian school bag which held three maize cobs, a small bottle of water, three dog-eared exercise books and three chewed pencils. They hugged their mother tightly as they left for school on that fateful day.

Their journey usually took about fifteen minutes along a rugged track leading to a small, roughly built school house surrounded on three sides by banana trees interspersed with the odd self-seeded maize plants. This morning they took the longer and, hopefully, safer route through the forest to avoid meeting anyone.

A nervous and diminished group of school children sat down on their wooden benches at the normal time of 7.30am and, although the sun's early rays penetrated the large apertures in a room built of rukarakara (sandstone blocks, mud and sand) it felt cold and the children fidgeted as they whispered to one another. The two teachers stood close together well away from the door opening talking in hushed tones, their furtive glances evoking a tense atmosphere which was transmitted to the children.

The sound of gunfire made the children jump, several screamed and most ran to the rear of the room as did the teachers. An open backed lorry full of what looked like soldiers, all shouting and waving guns and machetes in the air, roared past in a cloud of dust.

The teachers told the children to lie down on the floor and keep very quiet. This they did the only sound being an occasional stifled sob as one little child whimpered, 'I want my Mommy,' another, 'I want to wee.'

The children lay on their stomachs; Alphonsine was between her two brothers and lovingly spread her arms over their shoulders, no one else moved. Gunfire could again be heard in the distance as the sun slid behind a billowing grey cloud and cast the room into shadow and the prostrate children into a multi-coloured carpet.

A car drew up outside and a stocky male official stepped from the passenger seat leaving several other dubious individuals in the vehicle. A sprinkling of children raised their heads and one teacher sat up hoping this was the new tutor they had been told to expect by the deputy mayor the previous day

Neither teacher recognised the newcomer and both were reluctant to get up and greet him. The children, still on the floor, gave their 'new teacher' sideways glances as they shuffled and whispered between themselves.

They were instructed by the stocky official to stand up and form lines. This they did hesitantly, encouraged by their teachers. 'Many of you are to be moved to another building for your own safety so you must wait here until I return - there's nothing to worry about we'll take care of you.'

There was a sigh of relief from the teachers and the children relaxed enough to sit down on their school benches again as the visitors departed,

Alphonsine calmed her brothers, and those about her, by taking out her water bottle and placing it to the lips of her siblings and several other children telling them to take just a sip to moisten their mouths which had become dry with fright.

The teachers decided to begin lessons so the children were divided into their respective groups and set work from the blackboard; school books and pencils were taken out and lessons began.

The sun seeped through the trees and the temperature began to rise as spasmodic gunfire again echoed in the distance making it difficult for the children to concentrate. Many of the twenty two children asked if they could return home to their families but were told they must stay where they were for their own safety. It was impossible for the children to focus on school work so they were eventually allowed an early break.

Most wanted to go outside and relieve themselves but this was more from fright than necessity. A teacher took groups of five children to the rear of the school building scanning the track for any movement while they squatted and whispered to one another. Several gathered large dry leaves to wipe themselves. There was no toilet paper, flush toilets or taps that turned, besides, water was for drinking not for wasting on washing hands.

When all had returned to the classroom Alphonsine took out the maize cobs and gave one to each of her brothers. Several of the other children looked on longingly, they had nothing to eat or drink, so the three maize cobs were broken into smaller pieces and distributed as was the little food other children had brought with them. Some had a banana or avocado, others had a maize cob, but very few had water. The little thumbs of those children with maize worked feverishly on the individual pea sized kernels extracting them in twos and threes from the cob before transferring them into their palms and popping them into their mouths. Others peeled their bananas took a couple of bites then gave the remainder to another child. Kernels from the avocados were usually smashed and consumed but today the children were not allowed outside again to find stones to use as crushing hammers.

Before noon a vehicle could be heard approaching. The children sat like statues, some with food or water bottles half way to their mouths. This time it was a covered lorry. Several rough looking men in scruffy clothing jumped from under the dirty canvas cover turning, as they hit the ground, to undo the tailboard.

Shouting and mini explosions could now be heard close to the school but the official, who had previously spoken to the teachers, had a priest with him and this calmed the situation somewhat.

The children were told to gather their belongings together and get into the lorry as quickly as possible but no reason or destination was given. One teacher was allowed in with them but the other, a Hutu, was hit in the back with a rifle butt and pushed back into the school.

The spinning hands of the driver on the steering wheel veered the vehicle in a half-circle creating dust clouds which partly obliterated the school room. The only sound and movement, as the vehicle lurched forward, was the noise from crashing gears and screeching wheels.

The children, most of them Tutsis, were rigid with terror especially the two peering through the torn canvas on the side of the lorry.

Chapter Twenty Nine

The worse aspect of war is not the danger
of wounds and death from the enemy,
but the submission of one's body and soul to
brutes and fools in authority

Martin Boyd

Alphonsine - Part 2

The lorry stopped several times and reported at road blocks en route where drunken Interahamwe mounted the rusted rear bumper, leaned over the tailboard and reached into the children who, by this time, had huddled at the back. They leered and jeered as they poked at the nearest children with rifle butts and machetes. During one stop the driver and his front seat passenger alighted and peed in full view of the children, lit cigarettes and nonchalantly lolled against the rear of the lorry talking about their previous night's exploits.

This macabre journey lasted for another ten minutes before the children were herded into a small unused thatched church devoid of furniture apart from two rickety wooden benches. The door was barricaded and thugs stationed at the window openings to prevent the children climbing out. Several children were injured when repelled with rifle butts as they tried to escape.

Although the interior was hot the children huddled together, wide eyed and terrified, and after a short time had elapsed one of them began to vomit, others wet themselves. Alphonsine, being the oldest in the group, walked slowly up to within a metre of one opening and, in a voice hardly audible, asked for water for the smaller children. After eyeing her up and down the reply was, 'We'll give you something Inyenzi but it certainly won't be water.'

The thug disappeared to the front of the building; the barricade was taken down from the door and two dishevelled hoodlums entered and pushed their way through to grab Alphonsine and take her outside. Some of the children tried to follow but were punched back.

Several of the Interahamwe had left their posts to see what the commotion was about and two of the older boys managed to climb through one of the window openings in the back wall and run into the forest without being seen. The remainder were too frightened to make any attempt to follow.

Alphonsine was dragged roughly to the edge of the trees and pushed to the ground, the boot of one of her captors resting on her chest, his right arm raised and bent with clenched fist as though having captured and killed a wild animal. Raucous laughter emanated from the remainder of the hoodlums and suggestions were made as to how they could teach the Tutsi inyenzi a few lessons that she had never learned in the classroom.

Alphonsine was abused and raped by all five of the thugs and was unconscious by the time they threw her back into the room with the other children who were, initially, too frightened to touch her bruised and swollen face. Blood trickled from the corner of her mouth and down her legs. Her brother was the first to creep up to her and endeavour to initiate a response but her eyes were closed and there was no reaction when he tried to get her to drink the last dregs from a water bottle.

Having previously seen a priest with their captors the children could not understand what was happening for they had been promised safety. Little did they know the treatment allotted so far was mild in comparison to the terror that was in store for them.

The noise of another vehicle could be heard above the laughter and guffaws of the Interahamwe guarding the children, and clenched fists were punched into the air as cheers drowned the noise of a vehicle's engine as it came into view. Even before it came to a halt it was surrounded and boarded and there was a slapping of shoulders and handing out of sorghum to those in the rear of the lorry. A bottle was passed through the window to the driver who took a long draught of the muddy, bland tasting liquid, wiped the back of his grubby hand across his mouth, then gave the sorghum to his mate in the passenger seat.

One drunken soldier had a small drum with him, made from a hollowed-out tree trunk and animal skin, decorated with beige hair from a dead animal. Others had alcohol of varying varieties distilled from sorghum and bananas - even a half bottle of vodka was produced. And so the party began!

A fire was lit in the small clearing in front of the church and the children could only pray that the priest would come to take them to safety. The drinking, singing and dancing round the fire went on for about half an hour before another vehicle arrived carrying several uniformed soldiers; it was time to complete their gruesome tasks before the sun went down.

Grenades and a small drum of fuel were extracted from the rear of the lorry and placed on the ground. A soldier climbed onto the shoulders of a crony, another passed him the drum as he balanced on the church roof. The bung was taken out of the drum and the liquid splashed liberally over the thatch the arsonist laughing as he threw the drum to the floor and jumped down into the group who cheered his demonic exploits.

Fuel seeped through onto the children. Some screamed, some froze, others ran and pounded on the barricaded door. Suddenly, there was an explosion inside the church; a grenade had been thrown through an open aperture. Several children were killed instantly, others were grievously wounded. Many issued high pitched, piercing screams as they tried to climb out through the openings only to be punched back, falling on top of each other in their bid to escape.

A couple of torches were made from dried branches and several Interahamwe proceeded to light the edge of the thatch which set ablaze immediately; dried wood and branches from the forest fuelled the now raging fire.

The drink sodden thugs danced around the building as it consumed the animate and inanimate, singing and cheering, waving their empty bottles in the air then tossing them into the inferno creating mini explosions as the remaining drops of alcohol found the flames. A gun was fired into the burning building, making sure there would be no survivors, before the roof collapsed and flames and smoke billowed upwards.

There was no sound from inside what little remained of the church; all was quiet apart from the occasional crackle and spitting from the funeral pyre. The scene of this heinous crime was now vacant the genocidal maniacs having piled into their vehicles and moved off in search of further victims.

The gentle breeze periodically fanned the flickering flames but their strength gradually ebbed and they finally succumbed to the lack of kindling leaving only a mound of smouldering, glowing embers and wisps of ascending smoke.

Chapter Thirty

'Pity is for the living, envy is for the dead'

Alphonsine - Part 3

It was the 6th April 1994 - two days after Habyarimana's plane had been shot down and the massacre of the Tutsis, together with some moderate Hutus, began in earnest.

The two boys had tumbled to the ground after escaping through the church windows and quickly found cover in which to hide. Having witnessed the massacre they lay paralysed in the undergrowth, hearts pounding, bodies pressed into the comforting cool earth and praying the soldiers had not seen them. Even though darkness surrounded them they remained hidden for several hours before creeping through the forest in an attempt to find their families. Holding hands they froze after every few steps petrified they would bump into Interahamwe or militia.

Faint voices could be heard through the trees and one of the boys thought he recognised that of a relative. Caution was thrown to the wind as they ran sobbing, with both grief and relief, into the arms of a cousin. Within a short time they were reunited with their respective parents and endeavoured to recount the terrible slaughter they had witnessed.

All the parents of the missing twenty two children had gathered together during the night not knowing what to do for, once the sun warmed the day, marauding gangs would be on the prowl again and it would be dangerous to search for their children.

Vestine would not believe what had happened to her children and the other pupils and the only way this could become fact to her was to go to the church - she knew this place of worship - she had prayed there as a child with her parents.

All the relatives wanted to search, not believing the boys' horrific account, but it was decided they should work in twos. Alphonsine's mother, and another father, took a tortuous route in an endeavour to avoid any murderers who may have slept off the previous night's hangover in the vicinity. Caution was needed when making their way for by this time the genocide was in full swing and it wasn't safe for a Tutsi, or even moderate Hutus, to be seen by the marauding gangs.

Nearing the church, as dawn was breaking, the smell of wood smoke and charred flesh reached their nostrils. They stopped and stared as the mound of now cooling embers came into view. Vestine attempted to dash forward but the accompanying parent placed a restraining arm around her, he was afraid a guard may have been left from the night before. He picked up a stout branch and, after circling the church under cover of the few surrounding trees, he decided it was safe to move. Clasping her hand tightly over her mouth, tears streaming down her haggard face, Alphonsine's mother tottered towards the pyre; a heap of charred bodies, the burnt bodies of her children.

With only well worn flip-flops on their feet and nothing to protect their hands and arms they tried to rescue their loved ones. The mound was still excruciatingly hot and the slight breeze circulating among the scraps of clothing and thatch caused them to re-ignite as they searched.

Vestine was told to go back to the village and fetch other relatives to help in the gruesome task of rescue. This she did and soon there was a large, but silent, contingent feverishly trying to identify their children oblivious of the fact that they may be caught themselves at anytime. With burnt hands, arms and feet and bodies black with soot and ash, the sobbing parents pulled some of the bodies clear.

Alphonsine was identified because of her height, she had been the tallest girl in the school. But the little ones could only be identified if a piece of clothing had escaped the inferno or because of lying face down their features were still partially intact. It was thought the child lying next to Alphonsine was her younger brother, her arm was stretched over his body as if protecting him.

The upper parts of several children had been partly protected by the bodies on top of them but their lower limbs had taken the brunt of the flames.

The scene was devastating as the remains of several children were laid out. Men tried to comfort their wives many of whom sat rocking back and forth whilst gently stroking the burnt bodies of what they believed were their children.

Vestine placed her hand on the charred face of her young son then suddenly screamed for his blackened eyelids flickered slightly and the cracked lips moved; there was still life in this black, burnt body. A homemade stretcher was quickly assembled from banana fronds and several men supported all parts of his body as they lifted him as gently as possible onto the litter. Unfortunately, his legs and thighs were so badly burnt slithers of flesh adhered to their hands as they slowly levered them from under the body.

He could not be carried to hospital twenty kilometres away because his stretcher bearers would certainly be caught and slaughtered; witnesses were the last thing the murderers wanted left alive. He was carried home and smeared with the traditional mud plaster used for burns after what was left of his clothing was cut away. No other children, apart from the two escapees, survived the pyre.

As night fell Vestine and her husband made their way to relatives in the Virungas and there, by some miracle, they and their two sons survived the genocide. The frail, burnt little body of the younger son was taken to hospital as soon as the FPR rebel forces took control in the area and atrocities gradually abated, the marauding Hutus escaping to neighbouring countries.

One arm and the lower part of the boy's leg had to be amputated, the other leg, his face and back were left terribly scared and these wounds would not heal.

He lived for three excruciatingly painful months.

The remains of all the children were finally laid to rest in a mass grave together with several local children found massacred and thrown by the wayside. Much of the ash from the funeral pyre was scattered in holes in which young trees were planted and lovingly tended. These are now strong and beautiful saplings which will give shade to the young of Rwanda as they grow sturdy and play, hopefully safe, and in their teenage years **never again** suffer the horrors of Alphonsine, her brothers and friends.

Chapter Thirty One

'All our dreams can come true,
if we have the courage to pursue them'

Walt Disney

Meeting with Kaz

I began this book with the tragic story of a young boy soldier and here I was, sitting in a quiet Rwandan village one Sunday afternoon teaching the children English, when a short, light-skinned, young Rwandan about sixteen years of age appeared. He introduced himself as Kaz and informed me he had heard there was a Mzungu in the village so had decided to come to meet me. He spoke a smattering of English and, after helping with the children for a while, our English class soon made progress with an English and Rwandan teacher on board. Although there was much laughter when I tried to speak Kinyarwanda I felt life would be much easier if someone could do a little translating so, before Kaz left, I suggested he came again another Sunday. This invitation was eagerly accepted.

He seemed an intelligent good mannered boy and, after shaking hands and walking a short distance away, he suddenly turned and hesitated for a moment before walking back towards me.

'I really wanted to meet you mother but also wondered if you would be able to sponsor me in order that I can return to my studies; my life is ended if I can't return to school.'

At this stage we already had twelve orphans at boarding school which meant paying for their school fees, accommodation, food, clothing, bedding, toiletries and stationery. Our birth control and water projects were proving successful and also needed future financing. We were only a small charity and already our funds were being stretched to the limit.

Chapter Thirty Two

'It is the human destiny to be free'

The New Pascal (H) - Part 1
and Charm

Charm – not his real name but I am unable to remember or even pronounce it so called him Charm - is my old and trusted night watchman. He is short and stocky, unable to read or write, but is meticulous when carrying out certain procedures and lighting a fire is one of them. His large rugged hands can effortlessly break branches as thick as my wrist but he has delicate and dextrous finger movements when selecting the kindling to start a cooking fire. He holds his little finger slightly crooked, as though holding a rare bone china tea cup, as he painstakingly selects each individual fragile twig and builds a miniature pyre before striking a match within its confines. He rotates slowly around the smouldering fire, fanning it with my tin plate, until the sculpture ignites and, within ten minutes, we have hot glowing embers on which to cook. The finale is spectacular.

I sat chewing the end of an already stubby pencil, thoughts having wandered precariously, as Charm and I finished dining together on maize, chipped potatoes (a real luxury) che and a shared muesli bar, when I noticed a boy of about eighteen years of age talking to some of the children farther down the track. Their heads turned and little fingers pointed in my direction.

The tall boy walked slowly towards me being followed by several of the children, eager not to miss anything. I stood up to greet him and we shook hands. In very poor English he said, 'Mon name are Pascal.'

My heart missed a beat for his voice and build were similar to that of Pascal K although he was taller.

I managed to compose myself as I invited him to sit down. We tried to converse in English but it was impossible and so reverted to French, in which he was fluent; it was now my turn to struggle!

Like Kaz - and half of Northern Rwanda it seemed - he'd heard there was a Mzungu staying in the area and wanted to meet her.

I apologised for our lack of food but offered to cook a maize cob, if the embers still had enough heat to brown it. The cob was placed into the hot ash and Pascal settled himself down on the bare earth legs crossed.

I could tell from which tribe he came by his features so trod very carefully when asking him about his family. In perfect French he said, 'I have no mother or father and live with a family in Ruhengeri as a houseboy. I have not attended school for a some time because I have no money and my work as a servant does not allow me much time to find paid work.'

There were thousands of orphaned children in Rwanda due to the genocide, war, AIDS, malaria, typhoid, and many worked as servants in exchange for accommodation and food until they reached an age when school fees were necessary. Schooling then became spasmodic or non-existent.

Pascal was quietly spoken and his disposition submissive. He continually clasped and unclasped his fingers occasionally cracking the knuckles – much to my discomfort.

We still had hot water in the flasks so made further cups of che into which both Charm and Pascal H heaped many spoons-full of my brown sugar transported from England. Rwandans love sweet che but so rarely can afford the luxury of sugar.

Charm turned the maize cob several times then fished it out of the embers with leathery fingers before blowing away the ash and handing the blackened delicacy to Pascal together with a few words in Kinyarwanda. They chatted for a minute or two then Charm, barefoot and trousers folded up to just below his knees and a jacket two sizes too large which reached his turn ups, decided he must take up his post as guard on the supplies delivered that afternoon. These consisted of two and a half kilometres of piping, fittings and cement with which we were to begin our next pipeline.

I struggled with general conversation in French for a further ten minutes, as Pascal shelled and ate his maize, before he stood up and said he must leave, he had to cook dinner for the family.

'I prepared everything before I left,' he said, shaking my hand warmly and thanking me for my hospitality.

I didn't see Pascal again for a while until I bumped into him in Ruhengeri market one Saturday morning. I was grateful for his offer of translating for, although the stall holders were getting used to my visits and elementary Kinyarwanda, Pascal's company sped the shopping expedition along considerably. I again issued an invitation for him to eat with me the following Sunday but also stressed a family planning meeting had been arranged for about 2.30pm. No one had watches or clocks so the actual starting time was questionable; lunch would need to be served by noon.

Pascal arrived in the midst of our meeting and the women went very quiet. I was sure they were not used to discussing anything to do with birth either with, or before, a man so I asked Pascal if he could entertain the children and I would see him later. Unfortunately the meeting went on for much longer than expected and by the time we disbursed Pascal had disappeared.

Chapter Thirty Three

'The real voyage of discovery consists
not of seeing new landscapes,
But having new eyes.'

Marcel Proust

The New Pascal (H) - Part 2

I had no idea where Pascal lived and his absence worried me so I was delighted when I met him on the road from Kinigi early one morning on his way to church.

Rwandan places of worship house many denominations and different structures and are usually full to bursting on a Sunday morning. The services are long - three hours or more - vibrant and loud. Fire and brimstone belches forth and if you don't think you are a sinner when you enter you certainly feel like one when you leave!

We arranged to meet in town after church if he could obtain permission from his foster parents; I wanted to know much more about this boy's life story.

I sat in a roadside café in Ruhengeri arms resting on a table which sported a sticky, brightly coloured plastic cloth. Passing traffic billowed blasts of black exhausts fumes, specks of which gradually adhered themselves to the sticky plastic - and my elbows. I ordered two Fanta and awaited Pascal's arrival.

He arrived at a run, sweating profusely, apologised for being late and downed half the bottle of Fanta in one gulp.

We sat for a while conversing generally and I explained how and why I was in Rwanda and told him a little about my daughter and grandchildren. I then asked if he would like to tell me about his family and when he was a young boy.

There was silence for a while as he sat with his head bowed. I could see he was struggling so put my hand over his and told him he didn't have to tell me anything he didn't want to or proved too painful.

Raising his head he took a few deep breaths and said, 'My Mom had my little sister strapped to her back and we were running......... running. There was gunfire and I couldn't hear what my Mom was shouting. Suddenly she went down; bullets were going into her and my sister. I collided with them and collapsed on top of their bodies as they fell to the ground. Neither of them made any sound and I was so scared I couldn't move; the gunmen thought I was dead.' His eyes welled with tears as he lifted his right arm and wiped the corner of his eyes and his runny nose on the short sleeve of a nearly white T-shirt with the word 'Peace' written in red across the chest.

I could see Pascal was trembling and his tears were in full flow. I passed him a paper handkerchief and he pressed it firmly against his eyes until he became more composed and was able to continue.

'I don't know how long I lay on my Mom and sister; I was afraid to show I was breathing and still alive.'

He now started to sob and it was obviously too traumatic for him to continue his story so we sat in silence for a while and my thoughts returned to Pascal K and the fact that he, Alphonsine, Emmanuel, Dusabe, my sick baby, Hazika and so many other wonderful children were now part of my life and would always remain so. I had no doubt whatsoever that several more would be joining the fold in the none too distant future!

I finally steered the conversation around to Pascal's achievements and ambitions.

'I worked hard at school and attained a reasonable standard but don't think it's high enough to be accepted for university, neither do I have a sponsor.'

He explained he had not been to school for some considerable time as he'd been unable to earn enough for school fees. His work as a houseboy didn't allow him much time for anything outside the family with whom he lived and worked.

He struck me as an intelligent boy and both he and Kaz warranted some thought. I could promise nothing but realised there were now two more boys who needed help.

We finished our Fanta and went our separate ways promising to meet again as soon as possible.

During the next few days I gave much thought to this gentle boy's future and was wondering if our Trust could help him and Kaz achieve their goal.

I was anxious to get some idea of their educational standards so I could work out where we could send them for further studies and also assess if the Trust could afford two more students in higher education. I said nothing about sponsoring to either of them.

Fortunately, Pascal had made full use of any spare time having read avidly and been accepted for a few hours a week at Imbaraga Agricultural Commune, but his English was virtually non-existent and this would prove problematic if he was to obtain entry to the Ugandan university I had in mind.

They were very different; streetwise Kaz, gushing and exuberant; Pascal H was subdued, kind and thoughtful. Kaz's English flowed, incoherent but just about understandable, whereas Pascal's English was unfathomable. Conversation between us all proved laughable for Kaz knew no French, Pascal so very little English, me passable French and very little Kinyarwanda. We seemed to be translating for one another and getting nowhere fast!

They were bright boys. Pascal was three years Kaz's senior and, having experienced practical work at the commune and some higher education, badly wanted to try for university. Kaz had also missed several year's schooling but had caught up when in Uganda and was now ready for high school. Like Pascal, lack of funds were now his major problem.

I told them I would gather information on high schools and universities and would then see what the Trust could do about their further studies when I returned to Rwanda the following year. The breath was very nearly squeezed from my body and tears streamed down Pascal's black face; Kaz's Hamitic features sported a grin from ear to ear. Before I left Rwanda *they* had obtained all the necessary documentation for the Trust's scrutiny regarding their future studies. It was obvious our Trust would have to work harder with fund raising when I returned to the UK if these boys were to be included in our educational programme.

Chapter Thirty Four

'Teach us delight in simple things,
And mirth that has no bitter springs;
Forgiveness free of evil done,
And love to all men 'neath the sun.'

The Children's song
Rudyard Kipling

Christmas in Rwanda

I couldn't complete this book without a chapter on Christmas and New Year for most of mine are spent in Rwanda and, although a little austere, I make my subdued lists just the same. These lists don't include expensive presents, turkey, plumb pudding and bottles of wine but carrots, potatoes, bonbons, second hand T-shirts, worming tablets, eye ointment and anything else I can purloin to help and brighten the lives of children in the village in which I may be living and working. I also need to purchase yards of blue, white and beige material from a market in readiness for the beginning of the January school term and the producing of school uniforms.

With many children of varying ages and sizes at primary, secondary and high school, and one hopefully commencing university in Uganda, there was much bargaining and negotiating on the horizon. All our orphans needed school uniforms, shoes, books and every other necessity to make their austere lives bearable for the next twelve months.

Some of the boys seem to grow at an alarming rate, especially their feet. On one occasion, when arriving in a village, I found Bosco, after my seven month absence, about two feet taller and shoeless. He'd tried to squeeze his feet into well worn shoes ready for my arrival but it had proved an impossible feat. He did admit to playing football in them but I assured him that was not the reason his feet had grown so enormous.

Measurements, or better still the children, are delivered to my 'master designer' who has a trusty, old, black treadle sewing machine, box of chalk, pair of scissors and a rickety stool firmly ensconced on the pavement as you enter the town of Ruhengeri. I allow him to produce all the necessary garments on the understanding he gives me a hefty discount for mass production, plus all his remnants; the children love making rag dolls and on this occasion were to produce Mary, Joseph, Jesus and the disciples ready to take part in the promised Christmas celebrations.

Saturday, Christmas Eve, dawned and proved hotter than ever; the parched earth became ever more resistant to the rhythmic swinging blows from our hoes. We worked solidly from early morning until late afternoon to connect and cover the last stretch of water pipeline before our two day break.

We shook hands as I paid each woman her meagre earnings for her week's hard labour (the men were always paid by my foreman) before they wended their way home where preparations for individual celebrations and worship would begin according to their faith. Approximately 75% are Catholic, the remainder Protestants, Pentecostals, Anglicans, Seventh Day Adventists, Jehovah's Witnesses, Methodists and many other interesting cocktails, but most families are Christians.

I had promised the children we would sing carols and dance before they went to bed on Christmas Eve, consequently a host of children awaited me on my return to the village.

Sporadic village huts mingle with the odd banana and avocado trees together with patches of wilting beans and the ever present volcanic rocks. This makes it difficult to determine the limit of any specific village, the consequence being a horde of new eager faces arrived from neighbouring villages for Imbaraga's Christmas party. News spreads fast even though only some townies now have a mobile. There were sixty or seventy children from our village together with goodness knows how many 'foreigners' from farther afield; I had promised our village a Christmas Eve celebration and they were not going to let me forget it.

Many of the excited village children displayed their colourful hand-made rag dolls so it was time to erect a grotto. Dusty little black feet plodded back and forth with varying sized volcanic rocks balanced on their sweaty, cropped heads. (Everything is always carried on heads from sacks of potatoes to a pencil!)

On standing back to survey the newly constructed, semicircular shaped crib, made from various interwoven branches and a floor covered with dried leaves, I felt it needed some enticing extras. I had just the thing! One of my luxuries while in Rwanda is a long, white, cotton nightdress. During the day I may look like a bag lady but at night I try to regain a little femininity.

Unfortunately, the cotton nightdress is no longer very long - or very white - for I decided the lace from the hem would make a pretty decoration around the crib. This, together with several silver stars and moons cut from energy bar wrappers (the contents brought from UK and long since eaten) produced a veritable master piece and an enviable resting place for baby Jesus.

Our Christmas tree was formed from two stout branches which one of the older boys had managed to purloin. Another very proud boy tendered a battered plastic bucket into which we firmed soil and 'The Tree.' Before I left England my friend, Clive, had sorted through his old CDs. We had cut these into various Christmas shapes and punched a hole at one end. Each child threaded cotton through the sparkling rainbow decorations and these, together with green and gold tinsel and bonbons, were ceremoniously placed on the tree by a stream of unusually sedate children.

Night descends quickly in Rwanda so ordinary white candles, purchased previously in Ruhengeri, were placed at intervals in crags either side of a volcanic rock formation culminating in a plateau on which the home-made crib nestled. I picked up one small child so that she could place her precious baby Jesus into his crib with Mary and Joseph standing at the entrance to the grotto; the disciples were balanced precariously in vacant nooks and crannies.

With night approaching dozens of eager black faces were agog with quiet excitement; the flickering flames of a dozen candles responding to the constant gentle movement of many young bodies. The children were transfixed - it was a 'Silent Night' but only for a short time; it was a scene I will always remember.

There was no blazing log fire or brightly coloured wrapping paper covering expensive presents under our tree; no cosy armchair in which to flop after a hearty meal of roast turkey and mince pies. Bare bottoms squatted on bare earth; varying sized plastic mugs and rusty empty tins were brought along to be filled with sorghum, purchased in a cleaned out twenty-five litre oil drum from Ruhengeri the previous day.

I shouted 'Mceceke' (be quiet) several times and miraculously the multitude went silent in anticipation as I stood with an extended right arm held out about three quarters of a metre from the ground. Any child able to walk upright underneath my arm was instructed to 'Icara' (sit down) in a group behind me. I then lifted my arm to a height of about a metre and again the children of that height assembled into another group. This exercise continued until we had several groups of expectant, bubbling children waiting like greyhounds straining in the strips.

Pascal explained, in Kinyarwanda, I would sing some of my Christmas carols to them if in return they would sing their African songs, and dance for me. This caused an uproar of clapping and shouting; most Africans love to dance and sing and will use any occasion to do so.

I had written a very simple précis of the nativity story in English and, knowing the gist of the story, Pascal and Kaz managed to transcribe it into Kinyarwanda.

Silence reigned while the story of baby Jesus was narrated; our candles eerily lit the nativity scene and the faces of a hundred or so of my second family.

Having taught Pascal 'Silent Night' and a couple of verses of 'Once in Royal David's City' we sang these carols to the children and they, in turn, entertained me with their melodic descants. They sang their little hearts out especially when they saw how much I loved one special song – 'Africa'which they repeated over and over again.

The singing very soon developed into a crescendo, which I'm sure could be heard in Kigali, and we had turned into a troupe of whirling Dervishes as supple, young, boneless African bodies, governed as though by a strong breeze, swayed sideways, forwards, downwards, upwards, arms and fingers undulating and always with such finesse and artistry. They also have a way of rolling their heads very, very quickly in a half circle first to the right and then to the left which, when the adult 'lion dancers' don their special 'manes,' is most effective. It was only when the clouds of dust from the stamping feet began to choke our dry throats, and our vision diminished to but a few centimetres, I brought the dancing to an end.

The moon looked so near and large this particular Christmas Eve we decided to try and touch it. The word 'touch' was emphasized,

'We don't want to hurt the man in the moon do we?' (I pointed out a face which was clearly visible) to which there was a frantic shaking of heads and resounding chorus of 'Oyaaaaaaa' ('Noooooooo').

A line was drawn in the baked earth behind which the expectant multitude awaited.

Rimwi, kabiri , GO!' I shouted.

The children surged forward; a mob of jumping kangaroos; arms and fingers stretched to the limit above jostling heads, all shouting greetings to their new friend. I was assured by a youngster I'd scraped up off the ground and lifted on high that he was stroking Mr Moon's cheek. 'His nose feels like wool,' shouted another and, after the ebullicnce gradually subsided, several were sure his eyes had closed as they touched them, 'Very gently,' I was assured. This new friend was prevailed upon to come and join us several times until a friendly cloud slowly rolled across the night sky and I was able to tell the children Mr Moon had instructed the biggest star to cover him with a blanket, he was going to sleep. No doubt Mr Moon will think carefully in future about attending a party where unscheduled games take place!

At 7.30pm the time arrived for the children to return to their homes with their parents many of whom had joined our celebrations. They slowly disappeared into the darkness of the forest singing, waving, skipping, laughing elves and nymphs of the night. I prayed they would all have pleasant dreams even though their tummies were empty, their clothes in rags and there would be no visit from Father Christmas.

The moon removed his blanket, no doubt relieved that the party was over; it beamed large and full in an unforgettable midnight blue sky. I turned to say goodnight to the sleepy mountains whose constant, undulating summits formed a backdrop to the now hushed village. Sabinyo's jagged peaks jutted towards the clear night ski resembling the massive, uneven, black teeth of a laughing monster who had, I hoped, enjoyed the evening's entertainment. I heaved a sigh of relief to think the day had come to a wonderful end and I could sleep for the next eight hours.

A cold, but sweaty little hand slipped into mine; it clasped it with a firm grip and a timid little voice said, 'Don't leave me Deli.' The waif turned and stood before me holding up a leg for inspection, 'My leg hurts.'

I scooped the featherweight bundle into my arms and carried it the few yards to my dwelling where I lit a candle and inspected the offending limb. The wound was superficial, a mere scratch; the little body wanted love, warmth, food, company, comfort for at least one night of her stark existence.

I wiped the scratch, dressed it with a sticking plaster, touched thumbs and set about making a fire so that we could devour packet soup and maize bread together. Sandrine was but a shadow away throughout the preparations and I finally sat with her thin little frame snuggled close to mine as we settled ourselves beside the glowing embers of the cooking fire and dipped our bread into the steaming hot vegetable nectar. It was obvious she intended to stay with me so, hand-in-hand, we walked to my hut and prepared for bed. I cleaned my teeth but neither of us washed even though we were covered in dust from the evening's celebrations. After relighting the candle I found Sandrine a T-shirt and knickers to sleep in and, although it was only a camp bed, we fitted comfortably with my toes near Sandrine's shoulders and Sandrine's toes entwined around my knees. The unzipped sleeping bag covered us both admirably.

Before blowing out the candle we said our prayers. The child's prayers astound me for I think she thanked God for the lovely food she had eaten that night and asked that He make her a better girl who wouldn't fight on the morrow with her siblings over the tennis ball I had given her. She had nothing; no toys, shoes, warm clothes and yet was deliriously happy and grateful for her meal and my company - and the tennis ball! I didn't know where she lived and presumed her parents didn't mind her staying otherwise they would surely have returned to find her.

Charm, my night watchman woke me from a deep sleep, 'Deli, Deli, abashyitsi, abashyitsi.' I brought my arm from under the sleeping bag and ran a hand down the bed leg fumbling for, and finding, my tethered torch; it was 10.25pm. What did visitors want at this time of night? Conscience jetted in and my thoughts raced back over the day's events.

Hurriedly I pulled on a pair of trousers and jacket over my whitish night gown and tottered into the cool night air.

The visitor, a well dressed, middle aged Rwandan stood in the beam of headlights belonging to a 4 x 4 cruiser; two very well built male Rwandans stood either side of him. He moved towards me and held out his hand. 'Good evening Deri, I am sorry to have disturbed you so late but we have brought you and your children a Christmas present.' Beside my visitor stood a smiling bodyguard holding a cardboard box – far too big for chocolates I thought - but hoped! This he placed in my arms. It was heavy and I could feel movement inside so slowly bent down and lowered it gently to the ground. On opening the present I found two live cockerels and one hen!! They were for Christmas dinner the next day! I'm a vegetarian! I tendered my grateful thanks but declined to inform my friend of my eating habits.

Having boiled enough water to fill my two flasks before retiring for the night, I asked if my visitors would like che - hoping they would decline. 'Yes please, that would be most acceptable Deri,' was the reply as everyone sat down on a wooden bench in anticipation.

We chatted and supped che for some considerable time and I found myself drifting; I had been up since 5.30am.

My 'present bearers' left about 11.15pm and I think I was asleep before I actually climbed into bed. Sandrine hadn't stirred. In the early hours she must have tried, unsuccessfully, to lie beside me but the camp bed was too narrow and she fell out. Both of us ended on the floor during a spasm of giggling before I finally decided it was time to get up.

After a cursory wash and breakfast of bananas and pineapple, I told Sandrine she must return to her mama so, with a big hug, a cheery wave and two bonbons secreted in her hand – tennis ball tucked up the new knickers – she skipped off. From the expression of happiness radiating from her face one would have thought I had given her the previous night's moon.

The two cockerels, and one hen, were duly dispatched early Christmas morning............. to a nearby family with a reasonable fence of sticks and branches around their hut. We tied enough string round the cardboard box so that Bosco and I could carry it between us and the lucky birds were delivered to their new home with strict instructions they were not to be killed but kept for producing eggs and breeding purposes; a hen and cockerel to be given to another family should enough chicks survive the onslaught of the inevitable raptors.

Other presents left outside my hut Christmas morning included six potatoes, two maize cobs, honey in a rusty tin covered with a piece of rag, a dozen or so different coloured beans and a piece of torn paper on which letters were written, I think, by a child. I was unable to decipher the message but it had 'mana' in the text so I presume it was a Christmas card. I had explained to the children previously how we sent greeting cards to one another in England.

Early Christmas morning I sat with a mug of hot chocolate clamped between my cold hands wondering what most seventy-four year old grandmothers would be doing during this special day. Probably sitting enjoying TV with a slice of Christmas cake and glass of sherry placed strategically on the coffee table, or cradling a grandchild surrounded by its noisy siblings and oodles of toys and wrapping paper. Perhaps taking a well earned nap after cooking for the family. Not so in my case; lunch consisted of grated cabbage and carrot, sliced tomato, arrowroot biscuits and a mug of coffee.

An invitation to visit friends for the afternoon meant a twelve kilometre walk into the foothills of the Virungas to reach my destination. It was extremely doubtful there would be any type of vehicle on the road in, or on, which I could place my posterior. However, with hair washed in rainwater, finger and toenails scrubbed, wearing my best if slightly creased blue shirt and grey cotton trousers, I set off at eleven o'clock.

My friends were Seventh Day Adventists so had presented themselves at their church on the Saturday but other families were still attending their special Christmas Day morning services.

High, large town churches are built with many, many bricks, expensive stained glass windows and heavily decorated interiors. Others, in the country, have corrugated tin or thatched roofs supported with stout wooden poles and no walls. Beautiful descants, accompanied sometimes by only a drum, echoed into the ever receptive mountains as the Rwandans praised their respective Gods.

I received many invitations en route to join families in their celebrations so stopped to talk and give bonbons to the excited children. Everyone sported their very best, pristinely clean clothes. How they produce such shining apparel for special occasions remains a mystery to me. When I return to the UK my few items of remaining clothing is a pale shade of its original colour tinged with grey!

As I approached, the children were grabbed and their noses wiped clean of snot on their mothers' gukenyeras or the bottom of their T- shirts, the children squirming to free themselves from their mother's grasp; the supply of bonbons had been know to run out! On reaching Apollinaire's I think the world and his wife were there to meet the Mzungu. Relatives from both sides of the family had been invited as well as friends and neighbours. There were also several uninvited guests but all made extremely welcome. My succulent pineapple and packet of arrowroot biscuits (last remaining luxury, apart from coffee, from the UK) were added to the inevitable boiled potatoes, hard boiled eggs, rice and chicken and introductions were made.

Before eating we were all taken outside by Apollinaire to view the contented Jersey (I think) cow and her calf tethered in their stall, happily munching the chopped urubingo leaves most likely gathered by the children. It was obvious there was going to be some wonderful organic manure available.

We moved on and a door in the yard was opened to release a flutter of healthy looking brown hens who, we were proudly informed, produced enough eggs for the family's table and to sell at market. I had no doubt that at least a couple of these creatures were now cut into small portions and residing on the Christmas table. As the Apollinaires had six children both the eggs and hens would be a most acceptable bonus to their pantry.

Another door opened onto an outside pantry and kitchen and I don't think Mrs Apollinaire intended us to see this part of the household for a door in the house suddenly opened and she called something to her husband who immediately turned us round, shut the door and ushered us towards a well tended garden planted with potatoes and maize.

I had managed to gather some presents together and, returning to the house, I asked 'Mrs Apollinaire' to keep the children occupied while I hid coloured balloons, crayons and pages from a crayoning book outside. I am quite sure some must have been peeping for several went immediately to the hiding places. Nevertheless, the treasure hunt was a huge success, as was the blowing up of balloons and the crayoning.

My New Zealand friend, Baxta, had sent Pascal the money to purchase a second hand bicycle so I asked if he would come to collect me late afternoon on his trusty steed to save the walk home. His new foster home was five kilometres farther into the foothills so for him it was an easy ride downhill to Apollinaire's.

Pascal duly arrived, together with the two-wheeled transport, and was asked to join the festivities with the consequence it was dark by the time we waved goodbye to these wonderful, generous people.

I cocked my leg over the metal carrier clamped to the back of the bicycle, made myself comfortable on Pascal's folded jacket and away we went! Me holding firmly onto Pascal's flapping shirt tail with one hand and shouting 'Merry Christmas' as we sailed along waving to the many villagers out enjoying the balmy evening air. I laughingly wondered how many other septuagenarian grandmothers would be speeding along in the dark, on the rear of a second hand bicycle, without lights, through the very centre of Africa on this Christmas night!

Chapter Thirty Five

'Let them want nothing that my house affords'
Shakespeare 'The Taming of the Shrew'

New Year

I had promised to spend New Year's Day with the children of
Urugaga so my Pandora's box would again be opened and magic
performed................
New Year's Eve my visitor arrived but, this time, with a large
brown Hessian sack. This was placed ceremoniously on the ground
- a New Year's present! I stood back to see if the intriguing sack
moved, it didn't, so I stepped forward and warily undid the coarse
thick string; inside the sack were dozens of small fresh eggs. In
Rwanda eggs are an expensive luxury and rarely purchased by
villagers so they were a most acceptable present. After my visitors
left I kept a good fire burning and hard boiled all but six of the batch,
the remaining half dozen were my luxury.

I had again been exposed to more horrific stories of the genocide
on New Year's Eve and woke with a start early New Year's morning
with the sound of the beady-eyed crows' murderous claws pounding
a spasmodic machine gun rat-tat-tat as they bounced across the
rusty corrugated roof. It took several seconds before my stomach
left my throat and returned to its usual abode around the waistline.
The night had been a restless one after a nightmare involving gunfire,
machetes and slaughter.

Dawn had not yet arrived and my body and sleeping bag were
soaked in perspiration and, although the nightmare momentarily
disappeared, my mouth was dry. I fumbled for the elusive strand
harnessing the torch to the leg of my camp bed and ran an unsteady
hand down the short length of string to which the torch was still
securely attached. Matches found, I lit the candle residing on a
wooden chair near my bed and felt my heart rate return to normal
as the hut was bathed in a warm, comforting glow. I lay back for a
while then stretched before deciding to take a look outside; dawn
was breaking and the evil black crows had taken flight.

An opal mist hovered in front of the still slumbering mountains and a cold, damp, hungry little brother and sister huddled together waiting to see if I had any food left over from the previous night. Barefoot, and still in my night attire, I returned to the hut and found a couple of hands-full of cold rice, a banana and two hard boiled eggs, all which disappeared within minutes of placing them into the grubby outstretched hands. The water in my flask was still warm from the night before so I heaped two spoons full of chocolate powder into a mug, poured on the previously boiled water, and settled myself on a fallen log. My cold hands surrounded the hot mug and the comforting drink slowly navigated its way through my weary body. The horrors of the night slowly vaporized together with the mist which decided to allow the mountains' hazy outlines to appear in preparation for their daily bathing in the sun's welcoming rays. Needless to say I didn't drink all the chocolate for I couldn't resist the imploring eyes watching me. One white and two black faces each sported a neat frothy, chocolate moustache before the mug was turned upside down and confirmed empty.

Had any westerner visited the village early New Year's Day they could have been forgiven for thinking it was Easter for children began their day with brightly coloured, hard boiled eggs for breakfast - many devoured the eggs and crayoned shells!

Each child was also to receive an article of clothing, commencing with the forty-five pairs of varying sized coloured knickers for the young girls. In preparation for this difficult operation it was again necessary to form the children into groups in order of size and gender. Gender grouping is not always easy for all the children have shaved heads and have to wear whatever clothing is available. The boys often tried to hoodwink me, they knew I always began with distributing to the smallest first and were afraid the presents may run out by the time I got to them. Two boys decided they would endeavour to shrink in stature and join the younger children's group. With knees bent and shoulders hunched they hoped I wouldn't notice as they passed under my extended arm. I laughed and gave their bottoms a good slap which greatly amused the remaining onlookers.

At knicker distribution time I noticed one little girl fidgeting with her back to me. She surreptitiously whipped off her pants and stuffed them down the back of her T-shirt. I gave her a little pink pair with a bow on the front - for initiative. A T-shirt or pair of shorts were issued to the boys but, unfortunately, these soon ran out so, returning to my hut, I rummaged through my diminishing wardrobe and said goodbye to a few more tops, two pairs of shorts and one of my sun hats, this ensured everyone was kept happy.

There were faces I didn't recognise and felt sure they were from surrounding villages although I had stipulated this day was for Urugarga children only; I knew I would be hard pushed to cope with more than about seventy or eighty little people.

New Year's Day was supposed to be a holiday from work but it proved even more exhausting than Christmas. We had team games, usually girls versus boys, and always resounding hip-hip hurrahs for the winning team. Attempts at cheating required democratic intervention and, on several occasions, first aid had to be administered to knees and elbows.

Blind-folded children pinned a plaited rope tail onto a questionable sitting donkey (drawn by one of the talented older children) and this brought shrieks of laughter when the rope dangled from the creature's nose or ears. But....... the most hilarious team game of the day was dressing up for Catch the Train races, it had the children, parents and me shedding tears of laughter. In their haste to dress quicker than the opposing team, T-shirts turned into trousers; trouser legs appeared on arms and the boys had no idea what to do with a bra! I had, magnanimously, donated two out of my four knowing they would probably be in tatters by the end of the game. One boy put a bra on his head with the cups covering his ears, tying the straps under his chin!

The day ended with each child being given a page from a large colouring book and a crayon which they were allowed to take home, together with the traditional bonbon. Their laughing, happy faces said it all.

The night was cool and the pearly grey, full moon clearly exhibited its valleys and mountains as if in competition with the planet below. The never ending midnight blue sky, with its myriads of winking stars, equalled any celebrated artist's canvas; a comet streaking across the heavens added the last brush stroke to a masterpiece. The mountains were sleeping peacefully and I rejoiced in the fact that my nightmare had been but a bad dream; for thousands their nightmares had just begun - and for real.

Chapter Thirty Six

'Nobody would think that those who survived
and those who connived with committing genocide
could live peacefully in Rwanda – yet it is happening.'
Rwanda's Minister Charles Muligande

Pascal (H) and Kaz

Although Christmas and New Year festivities were over those children who had not yet returned to school were still in festive mood and eager to know what we were going to do. Most of them wanted kwega (study).

I had one further day before returning to work on the pipeline but I felt weary, both in body and mind, for it had been a hectic week and there was always someone wanting my attention. Oh! to relax in a bath full of hot water and sweet smelling bubbles with a glass of sparkling wine to hand and aromatic candles surrounding me.

It was nine o'clock Sunday morning and I had promised both Kaz and Pascal I would cook a meal for them before they left on their new venture, they were both returning to their studies. My Trust had worked extremely hard with fund raising, and sponsors exceptionally generous with donations, which meant we could support a further five orphans in their education.

Kaz arrived first and was given my Swiss army knife and a bag of potatoes to peel. The day promised to be as hot as ever and many of the children were stretched out on the concrete path surrounding the village commune, the last sheets from a thick crayoning book having been ripped out and one sheet given to each child together with a selection of coloured crayons. I had been teaching the little ones how to hold a pencil in preparation for when they, hopefully, commenced school.

Some of the older ones lay full length on their stomachs, top teeth sucking in their bottom lip, others sat with legs spread eagled and tongues protruding all diligently endeavouring to keep the colours flowing inside the lines of their varying pictures. Crayons were exchanged and the occasional scuffle erupted as a certain colour was grabbed from a neighbour in order that a work of art could be

166

completed. At intervals the coloured sheets were held high and shouts of 'Deli, Deli' wanting me to inspect so that I could see their progress and give words of encouragement.

We told the children they could take their beautiful pictures home to show their parents and this was greeted with cheers and squeals of delight as they handed in their crayons in readiness for the next session.

Kaz had been helping me with the children most of the morning and we had prepared the fire in readiness for the promised lunch. Pascal finally arrived breathless, as usual, and apologetic for being late; he had walked - and run - some twelve kilometres from his new foster home in the foothills of the Virungas his bicycle chain having broken. Kaz was jubilant for it was his last day before embarking upon his studies at high school. Pascal was very quiet but I thought we could deal with that situation after our meal together.

The main course wasn't exactly cordon bleu for it consisted of my last packet soup of questionable flavour the packet having gotten so damp the name of the contents and cooking instructions were illegible. Into this soup went the inevitable boiled potatoes, 'farty' beans, onions and carrots. The dessert was my old time favourite and pièce de résistance - bananas sliced lengthwise, fried in a battered old frying pan then drizzled with wild bee's honey, decorated with a little ash and flavoured with wood smoke.

I did warn the boys they may find the menu a little rich but, with noses twitching and hands rubbing together, I think they were prepared to eat anything I placed before them.

The whole saucepan of stew was soon consumed both boys enjoying two helpings. Then came the dessert - it was a huge success. When turning round to serve a second helping I found the tin plates obscuring both faces; there would be little need for washing up; the plates were licked clean! Pink tongues emerged and slowly curled around honey flavoured top lips. The backs of hands were drawn unhurriedly backwards and forwards across the corners of sticky mouths before also being licked, mimicking well fed cats savouring the last morsels of their favourite food.

We finished with coffee - from the UK - the boys, as usual, spooning mounds of sugar into the steaming hot liquid.

Eventually I heaved myself to my feet and invited the boys to join me in a walk. Several of the village children had been loitering in the background listening intently to our conversation, understanding nothing but eagerly hoping there may be a few titbits left over. Unfortunately, on this occasion, there was nothing but potato peelings and banana skins!

As we walked I felt that Pascal was still subdued so asked him what he was thinking about. He took my arm and continued staring at the mountains and the delicate wisps of cloud displaying an intricately patterned necklace just below their summits. 'I'm thanking God for the wonderful opportunity that is now before me. I pray the ground will be healed and we will see, in the future, only potatoes, maize and beans covering our soil instead of dead and mutilated bodies.' Kaz was less melancholy and slapping Pascal on the back told him not to be so sad, 'Just think what the future now holds for us - we must forget the past.'

As we wandered back to the village I wondered how could the human mind supplant the horrors and experiences of genocide, the holocaust, Sudan and Darfur. Everyone has to die but what has man in mind for future generations?

It was time for the boys to leave. I was surprised to see tears in Kaz's eyes and quickly responded; there was to be no 'Thank you' or 'Goodbye' just a promise they would both return, when they had finished their studies, and help Rwanda and its children.

Many of the children looked up and giggled as I hugged the boys in turn before they sauntered down the arid track with their arms about each other's shoulders. I prayed they would grow into men who, in the future, would work for the betterment of their country and **never again** experience the horrors of genocide and war.

Not the end but, hopefully, a new beginning

List of Abbreviations and Language

Abbreviations

FPR (mainly Tutsis)	Front Patriotique Rwandese (Rwandan Patriotic Front)
MRND (Hutu)	Movement Republicain National pour la Democratique et le Developpement
UNAMIR	United Nations Assistance Mission For Rwanda
MDR	Movement Democratique Republicain (Democratic Republican Movement)
BATWA (TWA)	Pygmy Tribe
RTLM	Radio Television Libre des Mille Collines

Historical Names

King Yuhi	Exiled king because he refused baptism
Mutura Rudahigiwa	Son of King Yuhi, renamed Charles after baptism
King Kigihi V	Son of Charles
Zaire	Now Democratic Republic of the Congo

Useful Rwandan Vocabulary

Gacaca	Weekly meeting of Peoples' Court of prisoners and victims or relatives
Mwami	King
muyaga	Wind
Inyenzi	Cockroach
Muraho	Greetings/Hello
Mwaramutse (ho)	Good Morning
Mwiriwe	Good Afternoon
Amakuru	How's things,what is your news?
Ni meza	Fine, good news
Murabeho	Goodbye
Murakoze cyane	Thank you very much
Murakoze neza	Your welcome
Yego	Yes
Oya	No
Uriziga	Make a circle
Icara	Sit down